THE

MORGAN
3 WHEELER

BACK TO THE FUTURE!

www.veloce.co.uk

For post publication news, updates and amendments relating to this book please visit
www.veloce.co.uk/books/V4763

First published in March 2015 by Veloce Publishing Limited, Veloce House, Parkway Farm Business Park, Middle Farm Way, Poundbury, Dorchester DT1 3AR, England. Fax 01305 268864
e-mail info@veloce.co.uk / web www.veloce.co.uk or www.velocebooks.com.

ISBN 978-1-845847-63-0 UPC 6-36847-04763-4

Readers with ideas for automotive books, or books on other transport or related hobby subjects, are invited to write to the editorial director of Veloce Publishing at the above address.

British Library Cataloguing in Publication Data – A catalogue record for this book is available from the British Library.

Typesetting, design and page make-up all by Veloce Publishing Ltd on Apple Mac. Printed in India by Replika Press.

THE
MORGAN
3 WHEELER

BACK TO THE FUTURE!

MORGAN

VELOCE

PETER DRON

Table of contents

Introduction

A series of strange events led to the creation of this book. The first of these was in early 2007, when I had one of those lightbulb moments, of which one should always beware. Influenced – and disappointed – by the cancellation of Volkswagen's exciting GX3 project, I suddenly decided, at about four o'clock one morning, that the Morgan Motor Company should start making three-wheelers again, after a hiatus of nearly 60 years.

VW's decision to abandon the GX3 was an opportunity missed, and an uncharacteristic outbreak of pusillanimity on the part of Dr Ferdinand Piëch, who is renowned for his ability to stop charging grizzly bears in their tracks, and convince lurking alligators to slide back into the murky river by staring at them disdainfully. The GX3 could have become the first volume-production three-wheeler in automobile history, and it might even have re-invented the sports car. Perhaps the German group will go back to it one day.

At that time, the Morgan Motor Company, or more specifically Charles Morgan, who then ran the show, was vehemently opposed to the idea of producing a three-wheeler, but this negative attitude changed dramatically a couple of years later. First, Steve Morris, then MMC's Operations Director, had a similar light-bulb moment to mine, and gradually set things in motion. After considerable reluctance, Charles Morgan himself became wildly enthusiastic, to put it mildly.

The new Morgan 3 Wheeler, put together in haste, was unveiled at the 2011 Geneva Motor Show. Reviews were ecstatic, although nobody outside the MMC had driven it at that stage. The level of public interest and advance orders overwhelmed the little Malvern company.

Only a year later, the production version of the 3 Wheeler, ready or not (and mostly not) was exhibited again at Geneva. Thus, the MMC (the definite article is obligatory) leapt into the fourth revolutionary change in its model line-up in its history; which is not many over a period of one hundred years. The others, in chronological order, were: the launch of the F4 (1932); the launch of the 4/4 (1936); and the launch of the Aero series (2000). There was also the Plus 4 Plus of 1969, but that was a revolution that failed.

The Morgan 3 Wheeler is an utterly ludicrous, impractical machine, that no sane person would consider buying. I thought about it for a year and then decided I had to have one, so I bought one. I don't even have the excuse that it was an impulse purchase!

After running it for several months, I had another light-bulb moment. Somebody, I decided, should write a book about this machine, and the extraordinary tale of how it came into existence. I decided, for one reason or another, that I should be that person. I submitted a proposal to Rod Grainger of Veloce. He replied promptly, offering a contract, so it is undoubtedly all his fault.

Many people have helped me. The MMC, including Steve Morris, Mark Reeves, Matthew Welch, and also former Chief designer Matthew Humphries supplied much assistance. Some of the MMC's suppliers provided me with some fascinating information, especially Mark Edge of ABT (the company that makes the chassis), and Shane Whitty and Jeff Bailey of S&S Cycle.

A warm thank you is due to Pete Larsen, the godfather of the modern 3 Wheeler, and also to Bill Fink and Lance Tunick, two serious car guys who have kept the Morgan flag flying in the USA for many years, through good times and bad. Conor Musgrave kindly gave permission for his photos of the M3W and the Liberty Ace together to be used. Also, thanks to Blake Marvin for his factory photos. My Morgan dealer, Chris Hatton of Marcassus in Toulouse, has been very helpful. Another person who assisted me, and who also played a significant role in the story, is my friend Andrew English of *The Daily Telegraph*.

Last, but by no means least, I should like to thank all the M3W owners who contribute to the M3W forum on the TalkMorgan website, the unofficial owners' club for the modern 3 Wheeler. Thanks particularly to those who have supplied me with photographs and information: Paul Jacobs, Calum Fraser, Donald Reid, Chas Saunter, Lee Cliff, Achim König, Jay Stride, Stig Svensson, Steve Harris and Brian Voakes.

Some 'members' of the forum, from Britain, France, Germany, Portugal, the USA and elsewhere, have an impressive range of engineering knowledge; one or two have made important contributions to the MMC's development of the M3W, continuing a tradition of useful feedback that has existed for many years.

By trawling through current and old TalkMorgan threads you can find almost everything you need to know concerning this strange little vehicle: what can go wrong, how to fix it, how to improve it. Despite failures and frustration, an affection for the machine shines through.

I have done my best to tell the story honestly, fairly and accurately; any remaining errors are down to me. I have a plausible excuse: if I had been allowed another six months or a year to do the research and the editing, it would have been perfect. This reminds me of something.

Peter Dron
Bargemon, France

Foreword

Charles Morgan used to say "Never go back," when asked about building a modern version of his grandfather's three-wheeler. I think I know why. Running a car firm, you have to be resolutely forward-looking, and while Sir John Harvey Jones did his level best to paint Morgan as an antediluvian institution, it was already in the process of profound modernisation, which harking back to pre-war three-wheelers wouldn't have helped.

But Peter Dron and I have always had a soft spot for the missing-wheel concept, even back in our days at *Fast Lane* magazine, and when he telephoned with news of Pete Larsen's trike, the Liberty Ace, I simply had to go and try it.

Why three wheels? Is it the imbalance that appeals to the driver, the purity that appeals to the designer, or just the danger? Richard Oakes, designer of the Blackjack Zero is a former Ford stylist and asks: "Do you really need that fourth wheel? Isn't it just superfluity?" Tony Divey, designer of the Triking, always said that to engineer a decent trike requires exploitation of the inherent imbalance rather than a fruitless attempt to cure it. Having driven, hill-climbed, raced and turned over a three-wheeler, I can certainly attest to the ache of fear in your stomach as you watch the inside front wheel dangling in the air on a corner ...

Getting to Larsen wasn't easy. This was 2008, and newspapers were laying off staff almost as fast as the banks were going bust. With zero budget, I bought the air ticket to Seattle to meet Pete, his partner Patti, and Cinnamon the dog, and drive the Ace. Before I left, I received a mysterious telephone call from Morgan. "Make notes," said The Voice. "We'd like to know what it's like."

As Dron documents quite brilliantly in the following pages, the rest is history, but it is worth saying just what a finely engineered and finished machine the Ace was. Lined up in Pete's wonderful 1930s factory were the initial batch of six machines, and I boggled at their perfection. I've never had the courage to tell Pete about the fate of the first car he sent to Morgan. Reverse engineering is what the industry call it, systematic destruction is another way of describing what happened to that poor car.

When I returned from Seattle, the phone rang: it was The Voice. "What was it *really* like?" Why does everyone think we lie in road tests?

Journalists seldom play a part in creating cars, but just as Steve Morris, Morgan's Managing Director generously credits that my road test of the Ace " ... certainly helped to make up our minds," so I should credit Peter Dron, without whose initial tip and subsequent support, I'd never have bought that air ticket to Seattle.

Whether history, owners, and/or the health and safety industry will thank any of us for helping create a car deliberately engineered and designed to exploit such a basic and inherent flaw in its configuration, namely one fewer wheel than normal, is debatable. Only Morgan could have done, it, however, and whatever the subsequent events, there's no doubt that the 3 Wheeler is a magnificent achievement. So hats off to them all, and to Peter for telling it like it was, and is.

Andrew English
Hydestile, England

Chapter one

Morgan, a suitable case for treatment

n the late autumn of 1974, on a pitch-black, moonless, foggy night, I was driving a heap of junk, a Chevrolet Caprice Classic to be exact, from London to Penmachno, near Betws-y-Coed, for reasons that need not concern the general reader. I arrived at a roundabout, completely lost, struggling to read the road signs, somewhere around the border of England and Wales.

Into this Hammer Horror set loomed a Morgan three-wheeler, with the top down, driven by an eccentric type with a fixed, slightly cadaverous grin. I recognized the combination instantly as the legendary Gerald d'Arcy Carr and the F4 he'd bought brand new, directly from the factory, in 1937. Although I had never really met Gerry Carr, I had seen him at motoring events, and I knew a little about him. This was the first Morgan three-wheeler I'd ever seen on the public highway.

Carr was by then an elderly motoring journalist with hair that had remained surprisingly jet black despite the passage of time. He had been employed for many years by United Newspapers, and had competed with his Morgan in numerous races, sprints and rallies.

When Gerry Carr died in 1995, he bequeathed the F4 to the Morgan Three Wheeler Club (MTWC), members of which can now hire it for a modest fee.

Some stalwarts of the MTWC were initially somewhat hostile to the new 3 Wheeler (the 'five-speeder'), but that has changed. Ross Herbert, guardian of the Carr F4, told me: "The officers of the club have always welcomed five-speeder owners on the basis that, as it is a 'Morgan' and a 'three-wheeler,' there was no good reason not to." Several 'five-speeder' owners have joined the MTWC, and some have started taking part in MTWC competitions (hillclimbs and sprints).

I never did discover what Mr d'Arcy Carr was doing out in the Welsh borders on that foul night. Anyway, I didn't consider the F4 a 'proper' Morgan three-wheeler, though I have since changed my mind.

Compared with the 21st century 3 Wheeler, it was quite sophisticated, and far more practical: its water-cooled Ford engine allowed cabin heating, and it had a proper windscreen, with wipers, and a hood (which, I am told, gave highly effective waterproofing). It even had doors. I greatly preferred the V-twin Morgan three-wheelers, in

Gerry Carr in his Morgan F4, which he bought brand new from the factory in 1937. The photograph was taken at a Morgan Three Wheeler Club meeting at Brooklands in 1995, the year of his death. (Courtesy MTWC)

The Volkswagen GX3, an exciting three-wheeler that very nearly became a production vehicle, but the German mega-corporation chickened out. (Courtesy Volkswagen)

particular the Super Sports with JAP (JA Prestwich) engine, though I'd heard rather off-putting stories about instability. I was told, for example, that it was advisable to have an acrobatic passenger to lean into corners, much like a racing sidecar passenger, though Bill Tuer and Hamish Bibby, the fiends of classic Morgan three-wheeler competition, seem not to need that. Maggie Tuer, who rides pillion, if that's the correct term, with both of them, ducks down into the cockpit and keeps the pressure of the volatile fuel at the necessary level.

Nevertheless, that image of Gerry Carr and his F4 softly vanishing into the pea-souper, direction unknown, stuck in my memory. In the early 1980s, in the car park shared by *Fast Lane* (the monthly magazine I then edited) and *Motor* (the weekly magazine of which I had previously been a staff member), there was a Triking. I knew a fair bit about Trikings, but this was the first I had ever seen close-up, and I was immediately struck by its exquisite construction and detailing. I tried to climb in but there was no room for my long legs. My first drive in a powered three-wheeled vehicle would have to wait another three decades.

As I mentioned in the introduction, in the early part of the 21st century, the slightly daft idea that Morgan should recreate something like the old Aero/Super Sports suddenly struck me. Modern cars, I felt, although technically superb, had become steadily less interesting to drive, especially if one wished to keep one's driving licence.

Amazingly adhesive tyres combined with extraordinarily clever electronic control systems governing braking, traction and cornering had made driving simpler and safer. Engine performance had increased to a startling extent, and silky-smooth gear-changes could be made by ham-fisted halfwits in nanoseconds. Reliability had improved unimaginably. All of this, unquestionably, was progress ... but I felt that something vital had been lost in the process, even though not many people seemed to care.

It's not only that when something goes wrong you cannot make the damned thing work again with spanners, a screwdriver, tank tape, a borrowed nylon stocking, a bit of ingenuity and some swear words. (Nor, in most cases can the nice chap from the rescue services.)

ACE 7 at the Morgan factory in January 2010. Looking on are Steve Morris (left) and Tim Whitworth. (Courtesy Pete Larsen)

Everything has become unnecessarily complex. Therefore, it seemed to me, like a good time for a return to minimalism and simplicity. I am sure that Colin Chapman of Lotus would at least have considered the concept if he were still alive (rumours of his non-death were exaggerated, I think). And indeed, the spirit of Chapman lived on into the 21st century in the form of the Volkswagen GX3 (see chapter three), on the development of which Lotus Engineering co-operated.

If Chapman had been around, with his feverish energy and entrepreneurial spirit, he might well have been the man to push the Germans into putting it into production. And the Germans would have sold shed-loads of them and made a handsome profit, in sharp contrast with the absurd Bugatti Veyron, a vehicle aimed at adipose plutocrats with no grip on reality.

If VW was seriously considering this project, and that was certainly so, then it was obvious, "... as plain as the face on your nose," as John Watson once said on live TV, that Morgan should do a modern three-wheeler. The company had begun as a three-wheeler manufacturer, and had operated exclusively as such for more than the first quarter of a century of its existence. Whenever people think of three-wheelers, they think of Morgan.

I had the opportunity to suggest exactly this brilliant idea to someone who, I thought, might listen attentively. I had let myself in for an unfortunately asymmetric conversation, ie the person to whom I was speaking possessed more information than I did concerning the subject under discussion ...

Toward the end of Press Day at the 2007 Geneva Salon, the sun had set outside but the lights gave full daytime effect inside the show halls. I strolled wearily onto the Morgan stand and chatted with Charles Morgan, third generation of his family to run the company.

Charles was bouncing with enthusiasm, as is his style, about a

project called the LIFECar. This, however, did not press the buttons or flick the switches for me. I thought then, and still believe strongly, that, while the MMC needs to keep informed about developments at the sharp end of automotive technology, it should never attempt to set the pace; simply because it obviously cannot – it lacks the resources to compete against the big players.

Taking advantage of a brief pause in his well-rehearsed lecture, I abruptly changed the subject, remarking casually that now would be a very good time indeed for the Morgan Motor Company to start making three-wheelers again. More than 50 years had passed since the Malvern company, which had improbably emerged into the 21st century as the largest remaining independent car manufacturer in Britain, had abandoned the type of vehicle that had established it, to concentrate instead on selling marginally less bizarre four-wheeled devices to weirdos who enjoyed wearing deerstalker hats even outside the hunting season. That's the caricature view, anyway. Morgan owners are, in fact, an eclectic group, even if among them there are many eccentrics, some of them undoubtedly close to certifiable.

The first Morgan I drove was a Plus 8, in the early 1970s. The wealthy owner had supercharged the Rover V8 engine. It was phenomenally fast, though at that stage in its development it returned only about 4mpg. But that was not the worst of it. I hated the handling, which I considered not only outdated but borderline dangerous. Well, actually, I thought it was a bloody death trap. I drove a few other Morgans over the years, but never liked them much. However, I recently had a brief blast in a 'narrow-body' Plus 4; even without modifications, it was very nice.

Anyway, back to the weird world of three wheels ... The last Morgan 3 Wheeler to roll off the Pickersleigh Road production line in 1952 had been an F4, not significantly developed from that of Gerald d'Arcy Carr. At that time, founder H F S Morgan was into his eighth and final decade; the former railway apprentice ran out of steam in 1959. His grandson Charles was one year old in 1952. The man who took the dastardly decision to end three-wheeler production was Peter Morgan, son of Harry, father of Charles. In fact, at that time, this undoubtedly made sound business sense. Indeed, had Peter Morgan acted otherwise, the MMC might well not have survived. But times change; and now we return to the Morgan stand at Geneva, 2007 ...

I had caught Charles' attention; I am fairly sure that his lower jaw dropped open for a moment. He gave me a piercing glare, with at least one eyebrow raised, as if he suspected that I had already started knocking back the muscle relaxants or sniffing the metal polish after a hard day trudging around the show.

I learned later, by coincidence, and shortly before this conversation, that a newly-hired young apprentice (who still works for the MMC, by the way) had broached the subject of three-wheelers during one of Charles' patrician chats with the workers. The young man innocently asked if the company might make them again. The reaction was an aggressive, contemptuous outburst. Charles was politer toward me, but I am a few years older than him and I was representing *The Daily Telegraph*, a major national newspaper.

Andrew English (left), Motoring Correspondent of The Daily Telegraph, with Matt Humphries, then Morgan's Chief Designer, after the unveiling of the M3W at the 2011 Geneva Motor Show. (Courtesy MMC)

I ploughed on regardless, ignoring the still-raised eyebrow, and insisted that I was completely serious. I recommended that he should make things simpler for himself by buying the rights to the Triking as the basis for the new model, as Tony Divey, who died in 2013, was then beginning to wind down his business. Here I had dropped my second heavy brick. I did not realize, at the time of this discussion that Charles had already met Tony Divey some years earlier (see chapter three), and that the meeting had not gone well.

Charles clearly did not consider my suggestion about the way forward for the Morgan Motor Company to be the cleverest idea he had heard in the course of Press Day, to put it mildly. Although he was proud of his family's history (and indeed his first car when he was a young gadabout had been a Morgan F4), he had no intention whatsoever of getting back into three-wheelers; indeed, for a long time he fiercely resisted pressure from the MMC Board to do so.

Once he saw the point of it, after driving the Liberty ACE, he immediately acted, with his customary Tigger-ish bounciness, as gung-ho ambassador for it, which is really what he always did best

for the company. You may be wondering, what is the Liberty ACE? Read on.

The day that the scales fell from Charles' eyes was still a couple of years away. That early evening in Geneva, having said my piece to an unappreciative audience of one, I decided I was talking into Charles' deaf ear, and that it was time to slot into the tiresome traffic jam and crawl back into the city centre in first gear to start some serious relaxation.

A while later, my friend and colleague, Andrew English, was engaged in the complicated process of assembling a Triking from various boxes of bits. I helpfully suggested that he should put in a rear axle and add a fourth wheel, and call it the Fourking. I added that he might think of extending the chassis while he was at it, to accommodate tall drivers in greater comfort. Then he could call it the Fourking L. Was he amused? Not much. Actually, I was greatly enthused by the project, as you may have already guessed.

I forget quite how, but I later chanced upon the website of American engineer and designer Pete Larsen, a successful manufacturer of motorcycle sidecars for Harley-Davidsons. Based in Seattle, close to the Pacific Coast, Larsen had decided that he wanted a modern version of the Morgan Three-Wheeler Supersports of the 1930s. After examining what was available, he, too, homed in on the Moto Guzzi-powered Triking as the best contemporary recreation of this strange concept, so he had exactly the same sort of vision that I had. Pete, though, had the imagination, determination and engineering skill to make it happen.

Despite trying hard, Larsen had been unable to obtain a Triking. They are rare, they do not come up for sale often, and at that time production had more or less ground to a halt (though it has picked up since). In frustration, he enterprisingly decided to build the damned thing himself, not surprisingly using an engine of Harley-Davidson origin because that was what he was familiar with. He called it the Liberty ACE and, after a long and difficult development period, he began limited-series production.

The ACE looked impressive, so I sent a link to the Liberty Motors website to Andrew English, the Air Miles king. He was sufficiently impressed to arrange a test drive on his next visit to the west coast of the USA. He subsequently wrote an enthusiastic review, which appeared in *The Daily Telegraph* in February 2009.

The *Telegraph* piece immediately caught the attention of the Morgan Motor Company, in which there were by then already pockets of interest in reviving the three-wheeler, despite Charles Morgan's aggressively-expressed reluctance. At roughly the same time that English's review appeared, a motor industry specialist in the USA, Lance Tunick, who had already advised the MMC on various matters, suggested the possibility of converting the ACE into a Morgan, having been alerted to its existence by celebrated San Francisco Morgan dealer (and former official importer) Bill Fink, the world's most over-educated car dealer.

The chief advantage of a three-wheeler, in the view of Fink and Tunick, was that it would enable Morgan to start selling vehicles in the USA again. The MMC had for years managed to squeeze its cars through legislative hoops, often with help from the ingenious Mr Fink, but finally the point had come where regulations regarding accident safety and emissions could not be met without cripplingly expensive investment, despite the relative sophistication of the new Aero, introduced in 2000, with its bonded aluminium chassis.

Because it would be presented and registered as a motorcycle, a three-wheeler would not be subject to the same regulations. Note to pedestrians: do not step out into the path of a Morgan 3 Wheeler, especially mine. You will suffer some painful burns as well as broken bones. It is as wide as a car but it is not a car (I have the official papers to prove it) and it will more likely be your relations rather than you filing the insurance claim.

The *Telegraph* article seems to have tipped the balance, and Tunick was asked to visit Pete Larsen, test-drive the ACE, and report back. He did so and his report was highly favourable. Steve Morris

and his right-hand man, Finance Director Tim Whitworth, went to Washington State for a test drive, and then for intensive discussions with Pete Larsen. A deal was struck and the MMC acquired the rights to the Liberty ACE, which was subsequently taken to pieces, re-engineered and redesigned in Malvern.

The result of all this negotiating and development was the new Morgan 3 Wheeler, first shown at the 2011 Geneva Motor Show and put into production exactly one year later. It was a remarkably rapid gestation phase for a new model, perhaps in retrospect a bit too rapid. Well, let's drop 'perhaps' and 'a bit.'

Morgan tried and failed to obtain engines from Harley-Davidson. The American S&S two-cylinder engine is rather like a Harley in appearance and sound, but is not actually a Harley; for one thing the vee is at 56 degrees rather than 45. Drive from this passes to the rear wheel through a thing called a compensator (of which more later) and then a Mazda five-speeder, as used in the MX-5/Miata, and a cardan shaft to a bevel box, and then a toothed belt that turns a large-diameter sprocket attached to the rear wheel. A bevel box looks like a differential with one exit cut off, and it performs part of a differential's function, in turning the rotational motion of the cardan shaft through 90 degrees.

The Liberty ACE had a simpler system, using Honda's shaft-drive, which is theoretically preferable, but the primary disadvantage (especially for right-hand drive) was asymmetrical seating, with ample accommodation for one person on the left side, but only sufficient space for someone with a tiny backside, preferably tapered, on the right.

Pete Larsen was granted a licence by the Morgan Motor Company to continue selling the re-engineered and redesigned version of the car, if that's what it is, that he had created, and is now Morgan's agent in Washington State.

Steve Morris, who had joined Morgan as a 16-year-old apprentice in the Sheet Metal department in 1983, was appointed Managing Director in February 2013. The Board's announcement concluded as follows: "Charles Morgan will concentrate on his vital role as the face of Morgan internationally, promoting the brand and selling the Companies[sic] products worldwide."

However, this did not work out to the Board's satisfaction. Following an acrimonious family dispute over whether the terms of this new role were being correctly observed, in October 2013 Charles Morgan, while still the biggest single shareholder in the company founded by his grandfather, was ousted from the Board.

In June 2014 he was reported to be working on a scheme to recapture executive power by buying out his sister's shares in the MMC, with the backing of a consortium. Stranger things have happened on land and sea, but I have been told by someone not connected with the MMC that hell is more likely to freeze over before Charles' sister would sell out.

This was one of Matt Humphries' early renderings for Morgan's return to three-wheeling. (Courtesy MMC)

Andrew English's Triking in 2009. The Triking played an important part in the M3W saga. (Courtesy Andrew English)

An icon is reincarnated. (Courtesy Calum Fraser)

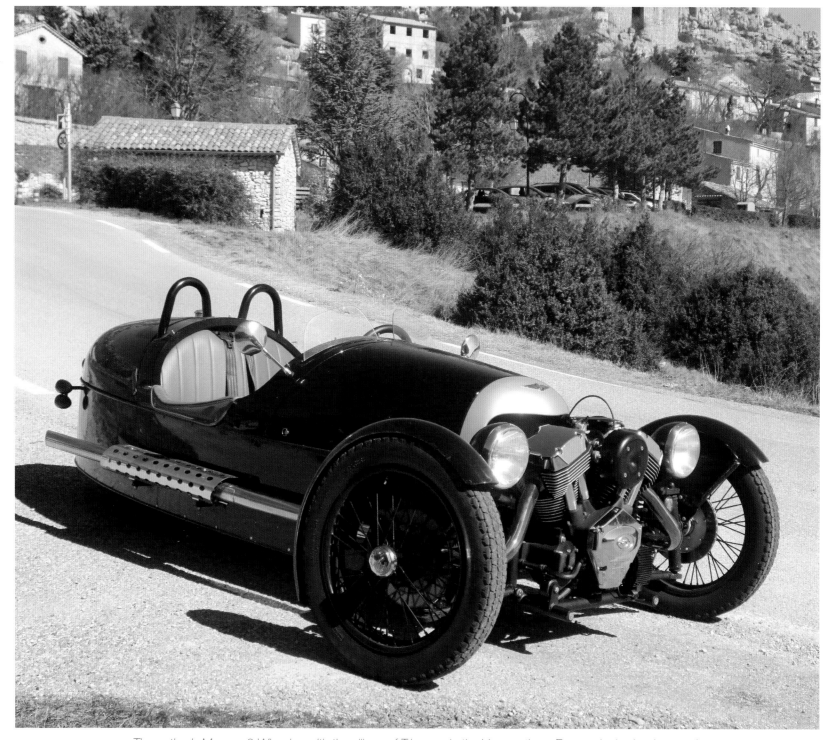

The author's Morgan 3 Wheeler, with the village of Trigance in the Var, southern France, in the background.

Chapter two

A brief history of three-wheeling

It is generally agreed by non-French motoring historians that the world's first motor car was the Benz Patent Motorwagen of 1885/1886. It was undoubtedly the first commercially available vehicle powered by an internal combustion engine.

This two-seater, weighing only 584lb (265kg), about half the weight of the modern 3 Wheeler, owed a lot to bicycle design, cycling having been a hobby of Karl Benz. The Motorwagen had three wheels, much like bicycle wheels. The front of these was steered by a tiller and the two rear wheels were driven via chains by what would today be called a mid engine.

Thus the first Benz had more in common, especially in its basic configuration, though not its intention, with modern American 'trikes,' or with the Trotter family's infamous delivery van in the British television series *Only fools and horses*, than with any Morgan three-wheeler.

Americans, perversely, refer to the M3W, which has two steered front wheels and a single driven rear wheel, as a 'reverse trike,' though Morgan three-wheeler enthusiasts ancient and modern assert that it is the Yanks (and Karl Benz) who put the single wheel at the wrong end.

In a series of scientific experiments, Jeremy Clarkson, the world-famous television clown, proved conclusively in his definitive review of the Reliant Robin that Karl Benz was lucky to have got away with it. Of course, in the 19th century there were neither product liability laws nor ambulance-chasing lawyers.

However, in one of many unusual and ironic twists in the tale of the modern Morgan 3 Wheeler, the existence of American trikes proved useful in the development of the Liberty ACE, which was without question an essential step in the story, though the Morgan Motor Company never went out of its way to acknowledge this debt.

Was that first Benz really a car? Definitely, according to motoring historian Nick Georgano's introduction to *The Beaulieu Encyclopaedia of the Automobile* (The Stationery Office, 2000), in which he eruditely argued with himself about what should be included in the authoritative three-volume set of doorstops of which he was Editor-in-Chief:

"A more difficult problem is posed by the distinction between a tricycle and a 3-wheeled car. Early tricycles, such as the De Dion Bouton, were no more than motorcycles with a third wheel, but from about 1903 a type of vehicle appeared which used the frame, saddle, engine and final drive of a motorcycle with two wheels in front, and a body, often of wickerwork, for a passenger. Known as tri-cars, they were still of motorcycle descent, but gradually the driver's saddle became a seat and the handlebars were replaced by a steering wheel, giving them the appearance of a tandem car on three wheels. With makes such as Riley, it is impossible to decide at which point they became cars."

Probably the first British attempt at a production car was the Knight. Built in Farnham, Surrey, from 1896, it was also a tricycle, based on the Benz model with one front wheel. It was produced in very limited numbers before the Knight company switched to four-wheelers and then quietly evaporated.

H F S Morgan was not the first engineer to produce a 'reverse trike.' That achievement should be credited to a gifted English engineer named Edward Butler (1862-1940). His Petrol Cycle was produced by the Merryweather Fire Engine Company in Greenwich (south London). It went on sale in 1888, though it is not clear whether anyone ever bought one. In fact, Butler had displayed his first prototype at the Stanley Cycle Show in London in 1884 – so, at that stage, he was ahead of Karl Benz, conceptually as well as chronologically. If he had continued, I am confident that he would have become convinced of the

In the driver's seat in this mysterious photograph from the early 1930s of a Riley Olympia is the author's father, T J Dron: surveyor, golfer, lifetime supporter of Booth's gin.

need for a proper braking system rather than his unusual idea of lifting the driven wheel when one wished to slow down. This was achieved by levering a pair of dolly wheels onto the road surface. The result of this operation would merely, at best, have been a slight reduction in the severity of the ensuing impact, preceded by a grating noise.

Butler, however, became understandably discouraged by the Red Flag Act, which imposed a maximum speed for self-propelled road vehicles of 2mph (3kph) in built-up areas and 4mph (6.5kph) elsewhere. Additionally, the vehicle had to be attended by three people, one of whom had to proceed in front of the vehicle waving a red flag. To the dismay of horse breeders, these restrictions were gradually relaxed from the 1890s onwards, but it was not until 1930 that rural speed limits in Britain were abandoned, in recognition of the fact that almost every motorist took no notice of them. In 1890, Butler gave up his promising and in many respects advanced project, and turned instead to the manufacture of stationary and marine engines.

Numerous other three-wheelers with two front wheels reached the market before Morgan. Among these were the Léon-Bollée Tricar of 1895-1899, the Swiss Egg & Egli (1895 onwards) and the tri-car of the Advance company of Northampton. In 1896, after a delay caused by a factory fire, Humber became the first manufacturer of series-production cars in Britain, and, like Benz in Germany, it began with three-wheelers; but unlike the Benz, the single wheel was at the correct end. Initially, these were Léon-Bollées built under licence from the French company. Lagonda built 69 Tricars between 1904 and 1908.

There was also the Riley Olympia, created in 1904. I have a photograph of my late father as a young man sitting in one of those, presumably in a museum or at the Riley factory, in about 1930. He looks very smart in his Gieves & Hawkes suit and his Lobb shoes, but I have no idea what he was up to on that occasion, and alas I did not see the photograph until long after his death in 1983; he was never a car enthusiast and I do not think that he ever owned a Riley. I imagine that when he sat in the three-wheeled Riley, which was six years older than he was, he regarded it as an amusing antiquity.

Three-wheelers, as noted by Georgano, steadily became more car-like, switching from guidance by tiller or handlebars to steering wheels. Then, from being car-*like*, they became bonafide cars: most early motor manufacturers that survived tended, like Benz, Humber, Lagonda and Riley, to switch to four-wheeled vehicles.

Thus, although H F S Morgan was highly inventive and imaginative, when he created his first three-wheeler in 1909, he was not being greatly innovative. Rather, he was swimming against the tide. This was probably to his advantage, as the motorised tricycle niche became more or less his to exploit and dominate. For some years in the UK, he had no serious competitors.

The Morgan 3 Wheeler was conceived chiefly as an economical car. Low running costs and a tax advantage made it an immediate sales success. Morgan itself states that "Harry Morgan can be regarded as the man who first introduced motoring for the masses." The claim is reasonable.

However, the vehicle's lightness also gave potential for sporting performance. This was exploited from the beginning: within weeks of launching the Runabout at the Olympia Motor Show in London, Harry Morgan himself competed in it in the MCC (Motor Cycling Club) London to Exeter Trial, winning a Gold Medal. At that stage it was a single-seater. Noticing that people were interested in his lightweight vehicle but unwilling to place orders, Harry Morgan asked questions and found out why. The production Morgan was adapted to have two seats; sales took off. He added a four-seater to the range as early as 1912.

By the outbreak of the First World War in 1914, Morgan three-wheelers had set ten British and World Records for various cyclecar classes, and won 24 Gold Medals in reliability trials.

There were numerous victories at Brooklands, including the first cyclecar race ever held. This was over a distance of about eight miles and took place on March 27, 1912. The following cars were participating in that race: the JAP-engined Morgan, driven by Harry Martin, an Autotrix-JAP, a Rollo-JAP, two Sabellas and two Bedelias. Harry Martin's Morgan Runabout trounced the opposition. Here is a report that appeared in *The Motor Cycling Magazine*:

" ... the red flag dropped and the race had begun. H Martin, on the Morgan was away like a shot ... at the end of the first round the Morgan had gained a big lead, and as Martin flashed past at close on 60 an hour he was given a rousing cheer ... There was no sign of his passenger on the machine, as he was cuddled up in the boot so as to lessen the wind resistance ... the Morgan was increasing its lead, and finally won easily at a speed of just on 60mph."

Morgan's prototype was a 7hp twin from Peugeot. All the early Morgans were powered by V-twins, mostly JAP, but many other engines were used over the years, including MAG (Motosacoche Acacias Geneva), Blackburne, Green Precision, British Anzani,

Blumfield, and Matchless. Some of these were water-cooled but most were air-cooled.

An old motor industry saying suggests that " ... competition improves the breed" (though if your Morgan dealer is involved in motor racing it can inconveniently close down the workshop from time to time). It can certainly improve sales, though, and from the early days it did so for Morgan, both at home and abroad, especially in France.

After the victory of a Morgan Runabout at the first Cyclecar Grand Prix at Amiens in 1913, Morgan three-wheelers became immensely popular across the Channel. Several cars were imported to France by various people, the most successful of which were the Darmont brothers. In 1914, 150 Morgans were sold in France, and for 1915 there were orders for some 500 more cars, but World War I brought manufacturing of non-military vehicles almost to a standstill.

Nevertheless, Morgan gained considerable publicity when the celebrated young Royal flying Corps pilot Albert Ball VC DSO MC bought a Grand Prix model. Ball may have coined the phrase " ... flying on the ground." He certainly compared driving it with flying. The Aero, introduced in 1920, was named in a tribute to Captain Ball, who had died in action in 1917. This was the successor to the Grand Prix model, although the two were produced side-by-side for some time. The more powerful Super Aero was introduced in 1927, and the V-twin three-wheelers became gradually better equipped, with front brakes, electric lights and starter motors.

Morgan had raised its annual production just before the 1914-1918 war to about 1000 cars. When the war was over the motor industry expanded rapidly, and Morgan immediately profited from this, increasing space in the Pickersleigh Road factory, which had been built in 1913, and transferring all production there from the original factory in Worcester Road. By March 1919, 20 cars per week were leaving the works. There was particularly strong demand in France, again assisted by sporting success. The frères Darmont made an agreement to build Morgans under licence. The resulting vehicle was called the Darmont-Morgan. The model range for 1919 was the same as in England. Some parts for the cars were shipped in from Malvern, others made at the factory in Courbevoie (Seine), on the western outskirts of Paris.

Remarkably, by late 1920 the Darmont factory produced 14 cars per week. Gradually the Morgan content of Darmonts diminished until the Morgan part of the name was dropped. Roger Darmont, the engineering brother (André mostly restricted himself to driving) designed and built his own bodies, built his own engines, and introduced all-new models, like the Darmont Spéciale (which could reach 100mph/160kph in supercharged form) and the Étoile de France. Production of three-wheelers ended in 1936, but in April 1935 Darmont had introduced the V-Junior, a four-wheeled car with three forward speeds and reverse. So Darmont added the extra wheel before the MMC decided to do so.

Another notable cross-Channel Morganist was the Anglo-French Stuart Sandford, who also began by selling Morgans. Finding that Darmont had cornered the lower end of the market, he designed and

Captain Albert Ball bought this Morgan Grand Prix shortly before being killed in action in 1917. In 1920 Morgan named the Aero model in tribute to him. (Courtesy MMC)

The iconic 1927 Super Sports Aero, inspiration for the external design of numerous subsequent three-wheelers, particularly Morgan's own revival model. (Courtesy MMC)

built a higher-quality (and far more expensive) 3 Wheeler, which he sold in small numbers until the war.

Between World Wars I and II, however, Morgan's most serious rival was closer to home, in the shape of the Birmingham Small Arms company, which had to do something to maintain turnover during the frustrating pause between worldwide outbreaks of military violence. BSA, having begun solely as a manufacturer of guns, had started making bicycles in 1880, and was involved in the motor industry from early in the 20th century, though its initial attempts at making motor cars before World War I had failed.

By the 1920s, BSA was possibly the world's largest motorcycle manufacturer, and it also began producing light cars in relatively small numbers.

In 1929 it added the Beeza three-wheeler to its range. This was powered by a 1021cc (62.3in³) air-cooled Hotchkiss-based V-twin. Unusually for the period, and well ahead of Citroën's Traction Avant, it had front-wheel drive. The Beeza could not match the Morgan's performance, but it was more comfortable, more practical, and better equipped. However, it was also more expensive, and an Austin 7, among other new small cars for the masses in search of mobility, offered better value.

BSA's three-wheeler remained in production until 1936, and undoubtedly influenced Morgan's decision to create the F4, which rather resembled the Beeza: both had the appearance of motor cars that happened to have only one rear wheel, rather than the hybridized motorbike look of the sportier Morgan V-twins. Nevertheless, Morgan chose the 1933 Motor Cycle Show at Olympia to introduce the four-seater F4. There has always been that lurking question: is it a car or is it a motorcycle? This has important consequences related to taxation and insurance.

The F4 retained Malvern's preference for driving the single rear wheel, but in other respects it was a big leap forward technologically. It had a pressed-steel chassis and the four-cylinder in-line, side-valve engine used in the Ford Model Y E93A, the water cooling of which allowed efficient cabin heating.

Just like the original V-twin two decades earlier, the F4 began as a sensible, inexpensive alternative to lightweight four-wheelers. In the late 1920s and early 1930s, this chiefly meant the Austin 7, which by then was well established, well developed, and with a variety of different body styles.

The sales slogan chosen for the four-seater Morgan F4 Runabout was "Motoring for the Million." The plural probably seemed unattainable even then, especially for a little company in Malvern, which, 80 years later, is still a long way from getting into seven figures for vehicles produced in its entire history.

Morgan's penchant for sportiness and demand from potential buyers was soon evident again. The F2 (two-seater) was introduced in 1935, followed two years later by the more sporty F Super Sport, renamed F Super in 1939. There was even a van version for 'Trotter-type' people who did not wish to topple over while making deliveries.

However, it was already evident that Morgan could not possibly

With mudguards (even if only of the cycle type) and aero screens, the resemblance to the modern machine is even more striking.
(Courtesy MMC)

hope to match the value for money offered by mass-produced vehicles which enjoyed economies of scale: it needed to stay within its relatively narrow niche market and offer something distinctive.

Car production stopped completely at Malvern throughout the Second World War, and the factory was once again turned over mainly to war work, though two car departments were kept ticking over by the MMC. These were the Service shop and the Spares department. Much of the other available space was occupied by the Standard Motor Company Aero Engines division, and the factory manufactured a variety of components for the war effort: carburettors, aircraft undercarriages, and other precision engineering work.

Sir Alan Cobham's company Flight Refuelling Ltd took over other workshops to develop wing anti-icing and in-flight refuelling systems, using a modified Handley Page Hereford bomber (a variation rather than an improvement of the infamous Hampden 'Flying Suitcase') located in the factory.

In 1945, many skilled employees returned from the Forces to rejoin the factory. Car production was resumed in 1946. In 1947, after being demobilised from the Royal Army Service Corps, Peter Morgan, son of H F S, joined as Development Engineer and Draughtsman. He had received a First Class Diploma at the celebrated Chelsea College of Aeronautical and Automobile Engineering in 1940.

The last twelve twin-cylinder three-wheelers were manufactured in 1946, using mostly a stock of pre-war parts, and shipped to Australia. The long period of austerity after World War II was fertile ground for a resurgence in demand for inexpensive three-wheelers, but Peter Morgan saw that there was more profit in making the Plus 4 (launched in 1950) and the 4/4, which had been introduced in 1936. The decision to discontinue three-wheeler production was made in 1950, and the last Morgan F-type left the factory in 1953.

However, the epitome of the pre-war Morgan 3 Wheelers was the Super Sports Aero, specifically aimed at competition use. It is this car that had the strongest influence on the design of the Triking, the Liberty Ace, several three-wheeled kit cars, and the 21st century Morgan 3 Wheeler. One particular feature of it was a beetle-back, whereas the previous Aero from which it had evolved had a more sweeping, pointy tail. The Super Sports was also wider and lower.

Later versions of the Super Sports carried a spare wheel on the tail, and, eventually, Morgan redesigned the rear into a 'barrel-back,' so that the spare was incorporated into the bodywork. However, although this improved everyday practicality, it destroyed the aesthetics, and many pre-war Morgan 3 Wheelers have been converted to have the more pleasing beetle-back.

Incidentally, aficionados of the older Morgan 3 Wheelers differentiate them by the number of speeds in their gearboxes. Thus, they generally eschew the terms 'V-twin' or 'F4' and instead refer to them as 'two-speed' and 'three-speed,' based on the number of forward gears available (reversing was not an option for the earliest Morgan owners). Using the same logic, they call the modern 3 Wheeler 'the five-speed.'

Chapter three

A saga of missed opportunities

The earliest three-wheelers, described in the previous chapter, came into being for reasons of simplicity, lightness, and low cost, particularly because of the lower taxes to which they were subject.

As stated, H F S Morgan really invented the inexpensive runabout for the ordinary motorist. Herbert Austin, with the Seven, merely made the concept more practical, and then Ford and others cashed in.

In the 1950s, Morgan opted out of this sector because it had no chance of matching the value for money offered by the larger manufacturers, and it was evidently unwise to go down-market to the fad for cheap 'microcars,' or 'bubble cars' as they were often rather derisively termed. These became popular in Britain with people on low incomes, but who were, naturally, keen to remain mobile. Many of these devices were manufactured in Germany, and had familiar aeronautical names.

In about 1960, the bubble car market imploded, and many of those companies involved in production of the, mostly ghastly, little vehicles vanished without trace. BMW, through its Isetta connection, was almost bankrupted by this sudden social shift, and was forced to re-invent itself in a hurry. The arrival of the Austin Mini is often cited as the cause of this implosion, and it's ironic now to ponder upon that, but in reality, the buying public, while still intent upon mobility, was less desperate than it had been.

In July 1957, Harold Macmillan, the British Prime Minister, had astutely predicted the demise of bubble cars when he announced that Britain had " ... never had it so good." Those who had not already done so decided that it was time to splash out on an extra wheel (or indeed two if you include the spare).

After this, three-wheeling became the preserve of daredevil racers, collectors of the pre-war V-twins, and a few specialist, low-volume replica builders. One or two others, such as Reliant and Bond, persisted with their perverse insistence of putting the single wheel at the wrong end.

There are still quite a few people engaged in the struggle to squeeze a profit from building ultra-low-volume sporty three-wheelers. For some reason, the early 1990s saw a surge among such creations: the JZR was introduced in 1990, followed two years later by the Grinnall Scorpion and the Aero Merlin. All three are still available at the time of writing. The Aero Merlin was developed from the earlier BRA CX3, and uses Moto Guzzi's engine, five-speed gearbox and bevel box, with a reverse gear added. It might have formed a useful basis for a new Morgan, but perhaps the most obvious candidate was the one I had suggested to Charles Morgan (see chapter one), the Triking; also Moto Guzzi-equipped. All these modern three-wheelers, especially the Triking and the Liberty ACE, were visibly inspired by the pre-war Morgan Super Sports.

The Triking was created in 1978 by Tony Divey (1930-2013), a talented ex-Lotus technical illustrator and racer of Morgans. It has a lightweight tubular steel spaceframe with alloy body panels and a glass-fibre bonnet. It is powered by a Moto Guzzi V-twin engine. Originally, this drove through the Italian motorcycle's gearbox, without reverse gear, but later both manual and automatic gearboxes from Toyota (including reverse) were offered. In a review of the Triking in *The Daily Telegraph*, of August 26, 2006, Andrew English related an amusing tale:

"Divey ... sketched the Triking while working for MAN [Volkswagen's commercial vehicle subsidiary] in Germany. In 1978 he built the prototype and decided to drive over to Norfolk and let his former boss, Colin Chapman, have a look, but the first person to emerge from the office was that year's world F1 champion Mario Andretti.

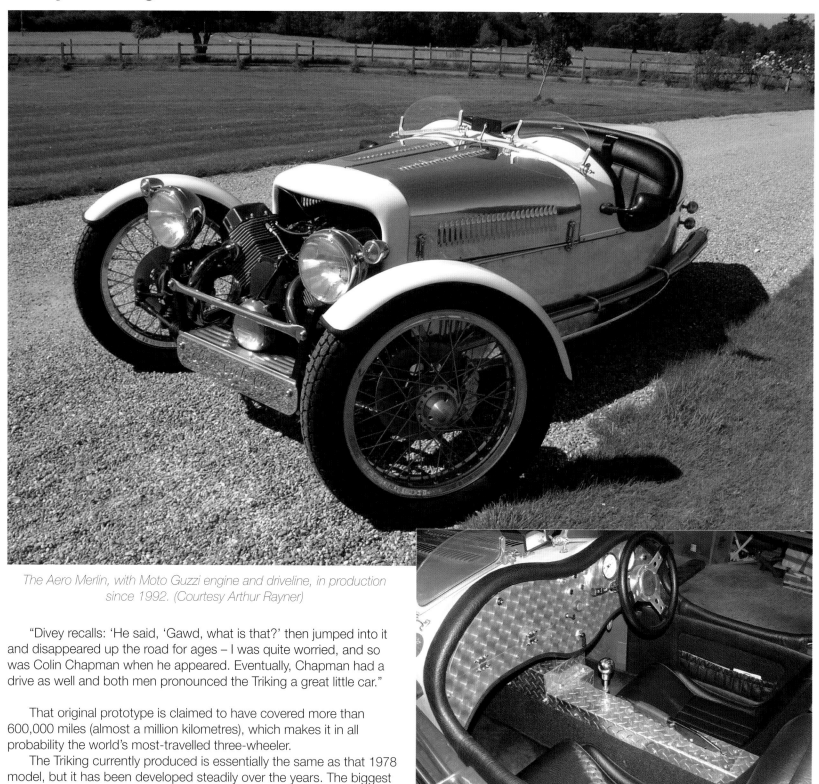

The Aero Merlin, with Moto Guzzi engine and driveline, in production since 1992. (Courtesy Arthur Rayner)

"Divey recalls: 'He said, 'Gawd, what is that?' then jumped into it and disappeared up the road for ages – I was quite worried, and so was Colin Chapman when he appeared. Eventually, Chapman had a drive as well and both men pronounced the Triking a great little car."

That original prototype is claimed to have covered more than 600,000 miles (almost a million kilometres), which makes it in all probability the world's most-travelled three-wheeler.

The Triking currently produced is essentially the same as that 1978 model, but it has been developed steadily over the years. The biggest

Aero Merlin interior, with circle-polished dashboard, a feature which also appeared in the Liberty ACE. (Courtesy Arthur Rayner)

Andrew English cornering hard in his Triking at Cholmondeley 2012. Notice the compressed spring and tortured tyre on the loaded side, and the mad, staring eyes. (Courtesy Andrew English)

change was in 1990 when Divey introduced a new tubular front end and a one-piece glass-fibre body.

The Triking, though highly regarded, has never hit high volumes. The total produced by 2014 is probably around 200. The company is now run by Alan Layzell, an engineer who joined as Tony Divey's assistant in 1989. In 2014, Triking was producing "... about 10 chassis per year, fully built or in kit form."

As I had suggested to Charles Morgan in 2007 (see chapter one), the most obvious way forward once the decision had been taken to create a new 3 Wheeler would be to acquire the rights to Triking from Tony Divey.

The more sophisticated, unequal-length double wishbones and correct geometry of the Triking would have prevented all the bump-steer misery, while the use of the Moto Guzzi engine and driveline, especially its bomb-proof bevel box, would have solved a lot of others (and I am told that if Guzzi had been approached properly it might have been a keen partner in such a project). Why did this not happen?

In fact, it could easily have happened, if Charles Morgan had been even slightly willing. Alan Layzell explains:

"By request, in 2001 Tony and I took a Triking to the Morgan factory. Tony and Charles had a chat/meeting and I had a look around.

"Charles appeared dismissive. He looked at the Triking we had taken – but did not drive it. It was not even unloaded from the transporter. I can't remember the exact words but in essence the outcome was Charles said something like, 'We would definitely like to do something with Triking but not at the present time ...' and/or ' ... the time is not right for us now.'

"Unusually (for him), Tony seemed much more pro-active and interested than Charles was. I remember thinking afterwards that clearly they had conflicting personalities."

A puzzling part of this story is why the invitation was extended. The obvious inference is that Charles Morgan did not start that process, but was obliged to invite Divey for a discussion and was in a position to prevent any kind of collaboration.

Layzell adds:

"Incidentally, we built a Harley-Davidson-engined Triking in the late 1980s. It was not very good, had terrible vibration and transmission problems. I feel the high torque and cylinder angle was not suitable for this type of drive arrangement – the torque spikes were too abrupt and destructive. It could have been made quite good but only with

The Triking-Morgan, a German-inspired project that did not reach fruition. The MMC played no part in this vehicle's creation. (Courtesy Arthur Rayner)

very complicated, involved, heavy and expensive clutch and driveline shock-absorbing components. I am told Morgan are now finding the same thing."

A while after the meeting between Tony Divey and Charles Morgan had come to nothing, there was, in fact, a Triking/Morgan project, but this had no connection with the MMC, as far as I can tell. It was intended to celebrate Morgan's centenary in 2009, and it was commissioned well in advance by Merz & Pabst, a large Morgan dealership in Nürtingen, south-east of Stuttgart. The original idea was an edition of 100, but then this was scaled down to three, one red, one white, and one blue. And then it ended up as one, the red one; and that was only half-built. Layzell explains:

"The dealership had a rough design of the Morganesque appearance and sliding pillar, etc, that they wanted. They sent a fitter/ builder/designer to work with us on it for a few months. After about a year of part-time work on it, the dealership seemed to get bored with the idea and halted the funding. They told us to keep or sell what was already built as payment for outstanding work.

"I knew the sliding pillar would never work as it was, so we roughly assembled it into a semi-complete project and sold it to an enthusiast who intended to finish it as a 'special.' I also made him a standard Triking wishbone front end. I don't know if he ever fitted it. As far as I know, the MMC had no knowledge of or interest in the project."

The one-off uncompleted rolling chassis, the red one, is believed to be somewhere in Germany.

So that was one major missed opportunity in the M3W saga. Another, equally unfortunate, involved Moto Guzzi. At an early stage in the development of the new 3 Wheeler, the MMC was not expecting to go into series production. Moto Guzzi was requested to supply a cost estimate for a batch of a couple of hundred engines and other

Merz und Pabst, the German Morgan dealer that commissioned the Morgan-Triking, specified sliding pillars: spot the mysteriously inverted spring.
(Courtesy Arthur Rayner)

components. Someone at the Italian company gave an estimate of how much the bill would be.

If only someone at Morgan had asked, "What would the unit cost be if we decided to make about 600 per year, for several years?" or if the Italian company had posed the question. My information is that Moto Guzzi, owned since 2004 by Piaggio, would probably have been delighted to be involved in such a joint venture.

Over the years, various volume manufacturers have toyed with the idea of three-wheelers. Several have appeared as motor show concepts, but it's important to note that there are several different types of concept car. Always, there is the opportunity for young designers and engineers to demonstrate their talent and originality before they are put in harness to tow less exciting but more profitable carriages into the real world, or to redesign cup holders. So, some concepts contain a few styling or technical innovations that may appear on future production models, but are never considered to

be production models in themselves. At the most desperate end of the spectrum, concepts are run up hastily because the company in question has nothing else to grab media attention. At the opposite extreme, but equally cynical, a manufacturer may show a car that is almost exactly, bar a few trim details, what you will be able to buy in your local showroom in a few months' time.

Among the more interesting of the concepts never intended for production was the Peugeot 20Cup of 2005. This had the 170bhp version of the PSA/BMW engine, a six-speed gearbox driving the front wheels, and with a big, fat tyre on a motorcycle swing arm at the back.

Finally, there's a category that might be entitled 'Unsigned-off statements of intent.' A fine example of this was Volkswagen's GX3. It was unveiled as a 'concept car' at the 2006 Los Angeles Show. The GX3 was not only a clever idea, and superbly presented, as are all the best show cars, but it was also very close indeed to being production-ready.

An opportunity missed – the Volkswagen GX3, powered by the Lupo GTI four-cylinder engine, centrally mounted. (Courtesy Volkswagen)

The German company was deeply serious about adding the GX3 to its model range. The main point of it was to exploit the 'car pool' lane laws in California: since it would technically be a motorcycle, the GX3 would be able to use these lanes, and would thus be highly attractive to commuters. But it was also an exciting and innovative sports car, with tremendous potential, and it was enthusiastically received by both press (though only one or two journalists had the opportunity to drive it) and public.

The 1255lb/570kg GX3 was powered by a Lupo-based four-cylinder engine mounted transversely behind the cockpit. This sent 125bhp to the substantial rear wheel/tyre combination (315/30 R18) via a six-speed manual gearbox, and, to keep costs low, a duplex chain.

Performance was promising: claimed figures were 0-62mph/100kph in 5.7 seconds, and a maximum of 125mph/200kph, combined with excellent fuel economy (46mpg or 5.2l/100km) and the projected starting price was an enticing US$15,500. There was plenty of scope for tuning.

Volkswagen put prototypes through a lot of development miles, and there had been considerable engineering input from Lotus, particularly in the design and development of the suspension. Various steering and front suspension components borrowed from the Lotus Elise were used.

In the end, the Volkswagen Board decided not to proceed with the project, causing widespread disgruntlement, alas. A rather unconvincing reason given by VW for cancelling the project at a late stage was that it needed to be produced by a motorcycle manufacturer, and the VW Group did not have one at the time. Well, it does now, so perhaps one day VW will revive something like the GX3 through its subsequently acquired two-wheel brand, Ducati. In fact, the real reason for the cancellation, I understand, was that the big German corporation was seriously worried about potential product liability suits, though it could probably have minimized the risk by setting up a semi-autonomous subsidiary.

It could have added yet another logo to the group's array of badges, perhaps by acquiring the rights to the Messerschmitt name. Or it could even have struck a deal with Morgan to build it under licence in new factories in England and the USA. An opportunity to re-invent the sportscar was missed.

Chapter four

The Liberty ACE

n 1999, Pete Larsen and his wife Patty, of Seattle, Washington State, on the Pacific coast of the USA, had, for several years, been manufacturing a retro-style sidecar to fit Harley-Davidsons. Pete recalls:

"I was casting about for new products and challenges related to our three-wheeled specialty. I remembered the three-wheeler which had fascinated me in the 1980s: Tony Divey's Triking. An ongoing dialogue with Tony about the possibility of importing his piece to the US was to no avail. By 2000 I began mocking up my own version of a classic British trike."

He adds: "My 'bible' when thinking of the project was the book *Three Wheelers* by Chris Rees. Quite a bit is devoted to both the Triking and JZR. I was more attracted to the look of the JZR but could also make out that it was pretty cobbled together. Both cars used borrowed front suspension uprights ...

"I had never laid eyes on any of these trikes, including a Morgan, when I started the ACE, and the wonderful internet was not yet a tool available to me for research: the Rees book inspired me in both positive and negative ways, as in 'what not to do.' Early on when trying to just bring in some kind of trike kit, I phoned both Tony Divey and John Ziemba [the JZ of JZ Restorations]. I could hardly understand a word the man spoke, but gathered that John had some deal going with a guy in Texas and was not looking for any other distribution here. The frustration and failure to make any progress with either of these guys was really the incentive to go forward."

The Larsens had no backers, They funded a run of six three-wheelers by using the future owners' deposits and the proceeds of their motorcycle sidecar business based in a beautifully restored

downtown Seattle workshop that has belonged to Larsen's family since 1925. These premises later became Seattle's Morgan dealership.

So, curiously, Tony Divey had created the Triking because he could not obtain a Super Sports and Pete Larsen created the ACE because he could not obtain a Triking.

"My car would, of course, be Harley-Davidson-powered, and hark back to the 1930s Morgans, particularly those modified for racing with their extra wide front track, low stance, and fragile-looking clockwork assembly up front. During my mockup/prototype phase, I was

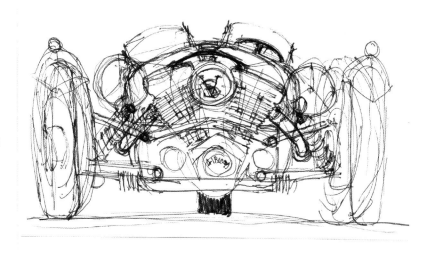

Above & overleaf: Pete Larsen's first rough sketches before he set to work building the Liberty ACE. The final vehicle remained remarkably close to his original concept. (Courtesy Pete Larsen)

"I well remember the winter of 2002, when all my weekends and holidays were spent in my pattern shop, deep in fiberboard and bondo dust! My Cycle-car first turned a wheel under its own power in 2004, and, while it was an exciting milestone in its own way, the first test drive was a huge disappointment: the steering was strange and there was unpleasant shaking and vibration. Drive train and steering revisions continued for more than a year – I disassembled the car too many times to count really. It required four drive adapter versions and a change of engine type and mounts to solve the difficulties."

fortunate enough to borrow and test drive a Triking for the first time, and the handling and performance potential of the thing was a revelation."

The ACE was to be of far more solid construction than those 1930s Morgans – or the Triking. The spaceframe is built of welded 1.5in/38mm diameter steel round tubes.

Going from a blank sheet of paper to having a road-legal vehicle that behaved as Pete Larsen wanted was a long, hard process, especially for someone working on his own, in his spare time. He soon ran into the problem detailed by Alan Layzell in the previous chapter:

With persistence, he got there in the end:

"Suddenly, almost six years since the project was begun, I found that I had a highly functional vehicle. I vividly remember awakening from a tiresome dream of endless work to find myself in the Cycle-car, miles from my shop, joyfully motoring down a country road without a care or problem; truly one of the best days of my life! I began to refer tentatively to the car as the 'ACE' for the way it made you feel while driving."

The ACE was powered by Harley-Davidson's 45-degree Twin Cam B engine, with four capacity choices, the 88in^3 (1442cc), 96in^3 (1537.7cc), 110in^3 (1688cc), and 120in^3 (1968cc). An advantage of this surprisingly sophisticated motor is that it has harmonic balancer shafts which reduce the vibration sent to the chassis throughout the

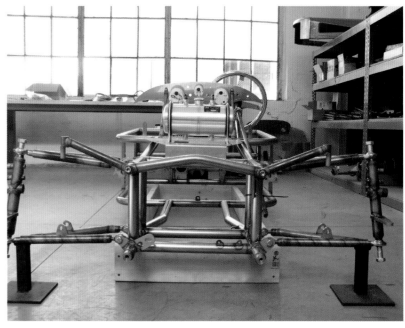

A Harley-Davidson Twin Cam B engine in Larsen's workshop awaiting installation. (Courtesy Pete Larsen)

An ACE chassis in the early stage of assembly. Although the Morgan 3 Wheeler's chassis is not identical, one can easily see that the ACE strongly influenced its design. (Courtesy Pete Larsen)

rpm band of the engine. These rotating eccentric masses cancel, to a worthwhile extent, the vibration generated by the uneven power pulses of the 45-degree V-twin. It also has an integrated flywheel. A disadvantage when you are installing it in a car, or even a sort of car, is that it has to be turned through 90 degrees, which makes the engineering of the transmission considerably more complex.

Larsen says that the effect of the balancers on the actual output torque spikes is not that great:

"In its motorcycle application, Harley still needs its compensator to mitigate those spikes. What the B motor did do for me was allow much more rigid mounting of the engine without the need for soft motor mounts. Without balancer shafts, the X-Wedge [in the M3W] absolutely required isolation mounting. After a couple of iterations of the motor mount configuration, Morgan finally settled on the four wide-based supports they put into production. These work very well to bring the vibration to a fairly pleasant level."

For the gearbox, Larsen originally looked at and rejected the Miata (MX-5) five-speed that was later adopted by the MMC. His objection was that he considered that it had "... a too large, non-removable bell-housing." He settled upon the Tremec T-5, originally manufactured by Borg-Warner and used in the Mustang four-cylinder and numerous other sports cars, such as TVRs.

Larsen explains: "The housing unbolts from the T-5, and I created a much smaller one for the ACE. I first ran a 5.5in/14cm racing clutch, but it was too hard to modulate, and I produced the next 12 ACEs with a revised, slightly larger housing and 7.25in/18.4cm clutch. In the end, my bell was just a bit smaller than the MX-5. Andrew English noted that the ACE " ... shifts like a rifle bolt." Larsen says that the M3W is "... softer-shifting and more user friendly." He adds, "The clutch, transmission and overall ratios in the M3W are beyond reproach in my opinion." I do not entirely agree about the ratios.

"Matching the engine to the driveline, as the MMC also discovered some years later, was one of the biggest development challenges. Getting the drive out of the V-twin to the flywheel and clutch was the most difficult task," says Larsen. It took " ... three years of testing on that issue, by itself, in my spare time, while maintaining another business."

Softening the fierce torque pulses of the big V-twin was the key issue. Comparing the Triking with the ACE, Larsen remarked (ominously for Morgan), "That Moto Guzzi unit has a pretty good balance. The Harley engine will eat transmissions, crack frames and destroy drive-shafts." It was necessary, as far as the transmission was concerned, to introduce something that would reduce this violence.

"Compensator," explains Larsen, "is a motorcycle term, probably coined by Harley-Davidson years ago. What I came up with, painfully, I might add, was a 'torsional dampening coupling.' I went through four quite different iterations to get to the production design. I ended with a simple, strong, silent, light design of my own which has never failed or given problems in the ACE cars." This was something that Morgan

Asymmetric seating was the disadvantage of using the Honda rear assembly. Obviously, this was unsuitable for larger-scale production, but in any case a motorcycle-sourced swinging arm was not an option for the MMC. (Courtesy Pete Larsen)

At this stage in assembly, the ACE still has its motorcycle tyre/wheel fitted, soon to be switched for a car wheel and tyre. Thanks to the single swinging arm, removal of the rear wheel on the ACE was far simpler than with the M3W. (Courtesy Pete Larsen)

The ACE production line. Note the wider tyres, on 16in rims. The Morgan's narrower front tyres on 19in wheels undoubtedly give it more of a vintage look. (Courtesy Pete Larsen)

underestimated in the development of the M3W. We shall return to that.

Moving further down the line, Larsen was able to use a solution which, for various reasons, was not open to Morgan. The ACE's shaft-drive is from the Honda GL1800 Gold Wing, but fitted with a car wheel and tyre because the dynamic loadings are different for car and motorcycle tyres.

"These are removed when automotive diffs are installed to create 'trikes.' I was able to procure zero-mileage units which would have

been cost-prohibitive to manufacture. The downside to this all-shaft setup is the severe offset of the drive-shaft toward the right. This would have nearly eliminated the RHD option, and at first Morgan mentioned using a BMW motorcycle final drive (see chapter seven) but I proposed the bevel/belt you see in the M3W which gives symmetrical seating. The Honda unit is quiet and trouble-free, of course."

The only disadvantage of using a rear motorcycle swing arm with shaft-drive is that it rises very slightly when you set off from rest because of the torque effect. Morgan's testing team particularly disliked this.

Together in Seattle: Morgan 3 Wheeler (Superdry edition) and Liberty ACE. (Courtesy Conor Musgrave)

Larsen had fewer problems with the suspension: "It worked very well right off the drawing board. I had a bit of bump-steer/roll-steer, but finally was able to purge all of that." For the steering he chose a Ford Mustang rack and pinion, shortening the track rods.

Larsen went to motorcycle coil/damper manufacturer Works Performance, which makes the sidecar damper units for Liberty Motors' sidecars, and " ... they produced the ACE dampers to my specs."

The Liberty ACE has 16in front wheels, which Larsen chose for dynamic reasons, and also because there is a wide choice of wheels and tyres in that size. "I was initially surprised at [Morgan's] choice of 19in wheels but now can't imagine it otherwise. A key here is that so many decisions were made on a cosmetic over functional choice." We shall return to this subject later.

Pete Larsen had thus added a Morgan three-wheeler replica to his range of sidecars, and settled down to the prospect of building them to special order, without expecting to be overwhelmed by demand. Then there was an unexpected twist in the tale, in which I played a small part, having alerted my friend, Andrew English, to the existence of the Liberty ACE. Here is Pete Larsen's description of what happened next:

Chromed cowl clips, standard on the Liberty ACE, have been adopted by many M3W owners frustrated by the standard system.
(Courtesy Conor Musgrave)

"Some time in early 2008, Andrew English of *The Daily Telegraph*, UK, reached me by email and expressed his long-standing fascination with three-wheelers, and suggested a visit here to test drive the ACE. I was delighted at the prospect of being published by the British press, but had no driveable ACEs at hand so could offer only a 'rain check.' By late in 2008, and after a fair bit of correspondence with Andrew, we were finally able to confirm a test drive for him in November. We met for the first time at the Seattle International Auto Show where I had ACE 1 and ACE 3 on display.

"The next morning we drove the two ACEs and two Trikings out to the countryside for a romp. Despite a wet road, all went quite well." The drive was punctuated by a visit to the home of Brian Pollock, a friend of Larsen's with a stable of Morgan Trikes, including a 1934 JAP Supersports. Larsen took a photograph of them in it and says, "In view of future events, it is for me an ironic record of a pivotal moment: soon after everything changed for me and the ACE.

"Andrew English's ACE review was finally published in February 2009. I read and reread the piece ... oh man, *The Telegraph* ... I was riding the wave! However, what came next was beyond my imagination: literally hours after Andy's review was published, I received a call from a gentleman who introduced himself as Lance Tunick of VCS, a consultant to MMC. Lance indicated a keen interest in the ACE by MMC. I had been eating a sandwich when I took the call and nearly choked!

The two vehicles share the same wheelbase but the Morgan has a wider front track. The ACE's body is longer and lower.
(Courtesy Conor Musgrave)

ACE number 13 and the Superdry in Peter Larsen's Seattle showroom. (Courtesy Conor Musgrave)

"Some weeks later, acting as an agent for Morgan, Lance visited our shop where he inspected some ACEs under construction and took a turn driving an ACE through the Northwest drizzle. Despite the rain and being attired only in a light Italian business suit and dress shoes, Lance popped out of the ACE beaming and declared it 'very user friendly.' Presumably the word got back to Malvern."

There was then a delay because, in 2009, Morgan was busy celebrating its centenary.

A key figure in the story was Bill Fink, probably the world's most over-qualified car dealer, with degrees from Yale, Oxford (hence his company name, Isis Motors) and the Stanford Business School. Fink used to be Morgan's importer for the USA, and he has been the MMC's dealer in California for many years. He has also installed Chevrolet Corvette engines in a number of Plus 8s. Here is his part in the story:

"Back in 2009, Michael Lally, a long-term friend of mine from Beverly Hills, was looking on the web for a battery-powered three-wheeler called the Teardrop that was used by Dominos Pizza to deliver pizzas in LA some years ago. During his search, he came across the Liberty ACE and rang me, suggesting I have a look on the web, as it looked very much like a Morgan 3 wheeler.

"I did, and sent Pete Larsen an email congratulating him on what he had built. I also rang up Lance Tunick, who had recently returned from a visit to Malvern, and suggested that he have a look at the ACE. He mentioned at the time that during his visit to Morgan he had commented to Charles while strolling through their car display that the 3 Wheeler was a car that could be sold in the USA as a motorcycle without all the fittings required on a car.

"Charles responded with three emails in one day, asking Lance if he thought Pete Larsen would agree to build cars for Morgan, or license Morgan to build them, or even sell Morgan the company outright."

In the end, Pete Larsen built 12 production ACEs and one prototype, so 13 in all. "I knew the end point was coming, by my contract with MMC to stop when the first production M3W was delivered to a customer. I am holding on to ACE 13 as my own example." Something like 130 M3Ws had been sold in the USA by the end of the first quarter of 2014, but some 2013 cars remained unsold. Liberty Motors had handed over more than 15 to customers up to that point.

It had taken Pete Larsen ten years of hard graft to get his project into production. The Morgan Motor Company examined every detail of it, and completely redesigned and re-engineered it, to the point that one might wonder why they went to the trouble of acquiring the rights to the ACE ...

As far as I can tell, there is not a single remnant of the ACE to be found in the M3W, though the dimensions are similar. Larsen's creation is 1in/2.5cm longer overall, at 128in/325cm, on an

identical 94in/239cm wheelbase, while the Morgan's front track is 1.5in/3.8cm wider, at 60in/152cm (as recommended by Pete Larsen). A key difference is in the overall weight: the ACE tips the scales at 950lb/431kg, while the M3W weighs 1157lb/525kg.

The ACE ended up as quite a rapid machine, with a top speed of over 120mph for the more potent version. The Morgan is intentionally a bit slower, partly because of the lower speed rating of its front tyres.

Larsen later recalled:

"Almost 60 years after the Morgan trike was put to rest, it would be resurrected with great enthusiasm and invested with modern technology, performance and reliability while retaining much of its original charm and fascination. While at the factory, I was introduced to Matthew Welch, the young engineer who would be given the assignment of revamping the ACE to Morgan's liking, including ease of manufacturing and service, maximum use of British suppliers, and many other requirements.

"The redesign, of course, would be done in CAD, not on a drafting board, as I had learned. The cosmetic aspects would be given the attention of Matthew Humphries, and I must say the results as I saw them only fourteen months later at the Geneva Auto Show are stellar: the new Morgan 3 Wheeler is not a rehash of a 1930s trike nor a quick makeover of my ACE; rather a well-reasoned and well-crafted retro-mobile: it has all the qualities I set out to deliver. Vintage appearance belies modern performance, just what I hoped to accomplish with the ACE, but here is the real deal and developed by Morgan themselves. As Andrew English wrote, 'Only Morgan could have done it!' I'll second that!"

English and Larsen were being gently ironic. Having reached a deal with Pete Larsen, the MMC then got the new 3 Wheeler into production within two years, despite a birdseed development budget in motor industry terms. One suggestion is that it was as low as £200,000, which is about the cost of a redesigned rear-view mirror at Ford or General Motors. It was an astonishingly rapid gestation.

ACE of Clubs – Pete Larsen at the wheel of his creation. (Courtesy Conor Musgrave)

Chapter five

Birth of the M3W

How much of the Liberty ACE made its way through into the 3 Wheeler that rolls off the production line at Pickersleigh Road? If you accept Morgan's presentation of the facts, the answer is: somewhere between not much and none at all. The American vehicle has never been mentioned in any MMC press material, nor on its website. However, although it is not obvious to the untrained eye, there is a lot of Liberty ACE lurking in the M3W.

Once the MMC had completed it centenary celebrations, Steve Morris, then Director of Operations, and Tim Whitworth (Chief Financial Officer) flew to Seattle.

"I was able to demonstrate an ACE", says Larsen. "Actually, it was a very good one in BRG and powered by a two-litre race motor. Steve briefly took the wheel for a few miles. The fun was brought to an end by a flat and I wondered if my hopes were going to go that way as well: the guys were tight-lipped. But no, we began negotiations that led to the complete buy-out by MMC of all ACE-related designs. In January of 2010, I flew to the factory, delivered ACE 7 for evaluation and signed an agreement with Charles. The Liberty ACE would morph into the new Morgan 3 Wheeler!"

Morris and Whitworth (the man who really runs the MMC), were convinced after their test drive that this was a project that the MMC should take on. They had been keen for some time for Morgan to return to its three-wheeling roots. They then had to convince the Board, and the greatest resistance to the idea came from Charles Morgan himself. While he was extremely proud of the company's past, he did not believe that a three-wheeler should feature in its future plans. Morris and Whitworth pushed on regardless, and decided very rapidly that the Liberty ACE was the best basis from which to start the project.

In January 2010, Pete Larsen personally delivered Liberty ACE No

7 to Pickersleigh Road, and he signed a reverse takeover agreement with Charles Morgan. This included a clause making him Morgan's dealer in Seattle. Thus, having failed to acquire a modern copy of the 1930s Morgan Super Sports and then built one himself, Larsen ended up selling his creation, or re-creation, to the Morgan Motor Company.

Even after this, Charles Morgan resisted stubbornly until everyone else had driven the car. Then, early one Sunday evening, he took the ACE out for a blast on one of his favourite roads ... shortly after which, Steve Morris got a very excited call on his cell phone. Charles said that the thing was fabulous. From then on, he embraced the project with his customary vigorous enthusiasm, perhaps even more than usual.

Larsen says: "That story was related to me at the Geneva Show in 2011 after the unveiling, and it is the one and only time Steve Morris has truly complimented me."

While at the factory, Larsen met the two Matthews: Matthew Welch, who had been nominated as the project engineer, and Matthew Humphries, the designer. These two were key figures in the team in charge of the transformation of the ACE into the Morgan.

The full team working on the development of the M3W consisted of: Mark Reeves (R & D Manager), Matthew Welch (Homologation and CAD engineer), Matthew Humphries (Head of Exterior and Interior Design), Jon Wells (Exterior and Interior design), Graham Chapman (CAD engineer), Chris Bridgens (Vehicle electrics and electronics), Craig Dolan (body/panel CAD engineer), Richard Harris (prototype build/ assembly engineer), Tom Morris (CAD engineer), and Mike Smith (multi-media design).

Mark Reeves and his colleagues began intensive evaluation of the ACE, driving it, making notes, discussing it and then dismantling it and examining and measuring every part. The development period was astonishingly short, by any standards. Some would say it was far too

M3W development team (left to right): Mark Reeves (Research and Development Manager); Graham Chapman (CAD engineer); Chris Bridgens (Electrics and electronics); Richard Harris (Prototype engineer); Matthew Welch (Homologation Engineer and CAD); Charles Morgan; Tom Morris (Trainee CAD engineer); Mike Smith (Multi Media designer); Jon Wells (Design); Craig Dolan (CAD Engineer); Matthew Humphries (Head of Design); Mark Cerrone (3 Wheeler Head of Production). (Courtesy MMC)

short, and even some Morgan insiders do not disagree, privately at least, though even privately it is not a favoured topic.

Three things made this accelerated creative process possible. The first was the Liberty ACE. The second was computer-aided design. The third was the Niche Vehicle Network, about which more later. The ACE had been designed entirely on a drawing board, the old way. The initial sketches of the Morgan were also hand drawn but all the detailed design work from then on was done using the CATIA (Computer Aided Three-Dimensional Interactive Application), the Dassault system that Morgan had been using since 2000 but which by then had been upgraded.

Matt Humphries recalls the frenetic design process: "I started on the project in September, and produced a final vehicle the following March for the launch at Geneva. It was fast."

The design brief, Humphries explains, " ... was to recapture the concept and feeling of the original car [the Liberty Ace] but to make it user-friendly for two people. We also wanted to incorporate the modern vintage feeling that we had built up with the classic cars: keeping the forms clean with engineered detailing and use of materials in a sympathetic way, such as the leather straps that hold the boot panel in place."

Big car companies have dozens of people working on the design

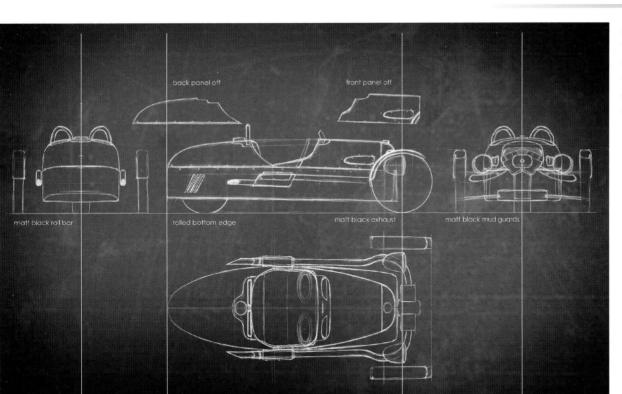

In this early rendering, rear side vents (introduced on 2014 models) and 'Brooklands' exhaust, now available as an option, had already been considered. (Courtesy MMC)

back panel off

front panel off

matt black roll bar

rolled bottom edge

matt black exhaust

matt black mud guards

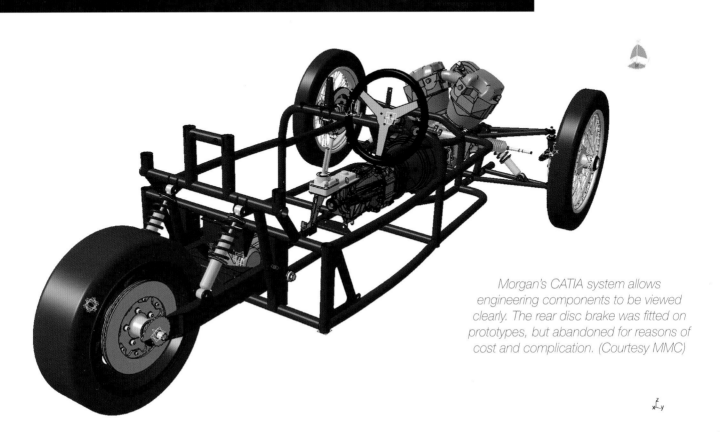

Morgan's CATIA system allows engineering components to be viewed clearly. The rear disc brake was fitted on prototypes, but abandoned for reasons of cost and complication. (Courtesy MMC)

of a new vehicle, especially such a bold leap into the past re-invented as the M3W, there will be dozens of people on the project, initially divided into competing teams and then working together. For the M3W, says Matt Humphries, "On the design side it was just myself and Jon as my right-hand man," though he adds that "Charles Morgan was also influential in the design."

Everyone seems to agree that Humphries and Wells, aided perhaps by Charles Morgan, did a brilliant design job in the time available.

The ACE had been constructed in an artisanal manner: it truly was hand-built, like Morgans of old. This new Morgan, on the other hand, although low volume, is a series production car, and it is manufactured in a manner of which Sir John Harvey-Jones (see chapter nineteen) would undoubtedly have approved: it is mostly hand-assembled rather than hand-built. Full details of this are in the next chapter.

The most difficult design challenge, says Humphries, was " ... the panel break-up, to make the vehicle look clean as well as work." He feels that the project" ... was design-led initially, but, of course, it was a 50/50 split. It was more like designing a bike, where the engineering is exposed to give an honest feeling to the design."

I asked Matthew Humphries what he would do differently if he were to start the project all over again. He replied, "Future-proof the vehicle for larger occupants." I had to look that up. Car designers are talented and interesting people, but they operate almost exclusively in the visual medium. Many cannot spell and they speak in a language that may become common parlance and intelligible to all 10 or perhaps 100 years hence. In this instance, he means that he would make it easier to move the pedal box to make life easier for drivers of different heights.

Matthew Welch was on the case well before Pete Larsen visited Pickersleigh Road: "I was first involved in the project when the existence of the Liberty ACE was brought to the attention of Morgan as a good quality example of a Morgan 3 Wheeler replica vehicle. This was about six months before we got an ACE in the UK for us to start to look at and test to see if there were legs in the project."

His first impressions were positive. However, "The ACE was the closest replica we had come across to a Morgan 3 wheeler, but there were a few things wrong with the look of the vehicle that distanced it from a Morgan, the main one being the position of the steering rack in front of the engine." This was felt by the team to prevent it from having " ... the nice exposed V-twin Morgan look."

Welch enthused, "To drive it was great fun but a little soft on the suspension for our taste. The noise and feeling whilst driving was really good fun though and it sold the concept to me and everyone else that drove it."

However, there was one thing that the team disliked far more than the easily-adjustable softness: "None of us that drove it liked the way it rose at the back under acceleration and pulling off. This was a nature of the shaft-drive system used on the ACE, and so we decided this would not be used on the Morgan design." Actually, as mentioned, there were more compelling reasons not to use it.

The chassis of the M3W looks slightly more substantial than the

ACE's, but both of them lack triangulation and this was a contributory factor in the early problems of the Morgan. The Liberty ACE has not suffered chassis cracks, while the Morgan's early problems in this respect probably resulted from the violent spikes of torque that the S&S delivers compared with the harmonically-balanced H-D engines in the American machine.

One might suppose that the MMC's sophisticated CATIA CAD system could have anticipated the flexing/cracking problems and avoided them.

According to Welch, the source of these is not the engine, as he explains:

"The chassis [of the ACE and the M3W] are similar at first glance, but in reality there are a lot of differences. There were some changes that look easy but are actually quite tricky changes, like moving the steering rack behind the engine. One of the things that was deleted from the ACE design was the headlamp mounting bar across the front of the engine. This was required for both styling and packaging, but it was something we missed to replace with gusseting on the first cars. It is not to do with the engine torque though, it is from braking forces acting through the upper damper and wishbone mounts flexing the front point of the chassis upper legs. You'll notice that the chassis now have much more triangulation.

"The frustrating thing for the development team was that through all of our testing we didn't see any cracked chassis ... it is always the case that no matter how much testing we do the customers always find something we didn't, which is a problem most manufacturers encounter."

The original brief for the entire project, explains Welch, was " ... to copy the Liberty ACE, including the suspension." However, the team soon encountered problems:

"When we got stuck into the design we quickly realized that there was very little that we would directly carry over from the ACE, including the suspension and steering.

"Moving the steering rack behind the engine created many challenges, but in all the suspension was a step forward from the ACE. The early design as such was tested and driven by people from the bottom to the very top of the Morgan management, and was approved and signed off. We had some issues with the coil-over supply, and this lead to some strange handling characteristics that quickly got turned into a general dislike of the handling.

"But the early suspension, or more importantly the steering geometry was very sensitive to change. The later design has more compliance and is not so sensitive to small adjustments, and pleases the masses more. At the end of the day we are trying to design vehicles for everyone to enjoy, not just individuals, so this ended up being the best option for us to introduce."

Although visually the ACE and the M3W differ considerably, and

Like the Liberty ACE, the Aero Merlin also has a forward-mounted rack, but this is cunningly concealed. (Courtesy Arthur Rayner)

although there are no interchangeable parts, Matthew Welch nevertheless concedes that the Liberty ACE was a vital part of the development:

"Without it we wouldn't have been able to prove to ourselves that there really was a market, and the possibility to make such a fun, enjoyable vehicle as the Morgan 3 Wheeler. Even though not so many details were carried over, it meant that we were able to eliminate some things from the Morgan project, and it saved us at least 12 months of development work ... think of the ACE as a one-off initial concept, and then the Morgan as the developed product from that concept.

"In terms of the styling and character we wanted to design-in, one of the photos we kept coming back to was one where the Morgan stand was being prepared for the 1937 Olympia Motor Show, with a great-looking 3 Wheeler on it."

The M3W development story was a seriously superheated affair, as Welch emphasises: "I suppose we first put pen to paper or clicked the sketch command in the CAD in February 2010. We built the first assembled cars and they were despatched for Geneva 12 months later, we got the first car started a few weeks after Geneva at the start of April, and I drove the first running car out of the factory gates to a local test area we used at the end of April 2011. We got there and then managed to break the centre drive within about five minutes of starting to test it!"

Note. That is centre with a small 'c.' Centa with a big 'C' did not come into the story until much later, alas.

Much of the testing was conducted on the roads around Malvern. As Welch explains, "There is nothing better than the real world environment to test something. But we also did a lot over at Millbrook Proving Ground, and the certification was completed with the VCA (Vehicle Certification Agency).

Not including Liberty ACE No 7, there were six prototypes before production began. Number 1 was the 'RAF car' (with roundels and other Air Force allusions) at Geneva. It was used for testing and is now privately owned.

Number 2 was the grey Geneva car. This was used to perform the ECE R12 frontal impact crash test, and, says Welch, it " ... is now in a sorry state behind our office."

Number 3 was a matt black car used for testing and a lot of the certification work. It is now the 'Grim Reaper' customised car on display at the factory.

Number 4 was 'the teal car' – used at the Goodwood Festival of Speed in 2011 to take potential customers for drives. It was then used for testing and is now owned by Steve Morris.

Number 5 was 'the sand car.' Mark Reeves used it to drive up the Goodwood hill with brave celebrities in the passenger seat. It was then sent to S&S for use for development engine work. By now it should be back in Malvern.

Number 6, 'the Dark Green car,' was used at the Goodwood Festival of Speed in 2011 to take potential customers for drives, then sold to a private owner.

Only 14 months after Pete Larsen left Malvern with a letter of intent from the MMC in his briefcase, though the company had to be nudged into this contract a few times, the new 3 Wheeler was ready for production. I should rephrase that: it was put into production, ready or not.

It was unveiled at 10.45am on Tuesday March 1, 2011, Press Day at the annual Geneva Motor Show. By this stage, the S&S engine was already installed. In exactly the same spot where, four years earlier, Charles Morgan had dismissed, almost derisively, my suggestion that his company should start building three-wheelers again, he now explained to the assembled Press why it was such a ripping idea.

Charles Morgan took care not to mention the Liberty ACE in his presentation, and the American vehicle was not cited even as a source of inspiration in any of the press releases from Malvern concerning the

The Morgan stand at Geneva. The 3 Wheeler received a vast amount of press coverage, and the little company was soon overwhelmed by advance orders. (Courtesy MMC)

Stealing the show – Matthew Humphries and Robert Gibson at the unveiling of the new M3W at the 2011 Geneva Salon; both have since left Morgan. (Courtesy MMC)

new 3 Wheeler. Many people were, and still are, under the impression that the MMC had literally started with a blank sheet of paper.

In the end, very little, if anything, of the ACE made it through to the Morgan assembly line. Or at least, there's nothing obvious at first glance, and all the components in the driveline are entirely changed from nose to tail. I shall return to this point later in this chapter.

Starting from the front end, apart from the S&S engine with its wider Vee, which is there because the MMC could not reach an agreement with Harley-Davidson, both the standard version and subsequent variations of the Morgan's exhaust system are unlike the ACE's pipes.

The double-wishbone front suspension designs are similar in dimensions and construction, but Morgan made some serious errors in deciding the ride height, and made a specific and obvious error in

the original design of the steering arms. The ACE's steering rack is mounted low down, ahead of the engine, while the Morgan's is higher and behind the engine.

Mark Reeves emphasizes Matthew Welch's remark that Morgan did not like the forward-mounted rack, feeling that it gave a " ... kit-car look." However, the ACE's suspension/steering layout looks geometrically sounder. Pete Larsen says that it would have been relatively simple to mount the steering rack behind the engine on the ACE, though he concedes that it would allow " ... a very small window to locate the rack." The ACE also has slightly wider, smaller-diameter front wheels.

The bodywork is not radically transformed, but again the details are changed. The dummy radiator of the Morgan, behind the engine, is wider and of an altered design, while its beetle-back is raised and its curvatures more complex.

One of the earliest cars off the production line, chassis number 13, collected from the factory by serial Morgan customer Brian Voakes. *(Courtesy Brian Voakes)*

The two cars both have what looks like roll-over protection, but the Liberty ACE's single hoop and the aesthetically more pleasing twin hoops of the Morgan share a flaw: they aren't braced, and without triangulation they would be inadequate in anything but a very low-speed capsize.

The two cockpits are very different. Most obviously, the Morgan's is symmetrical, and, therefore, suitable for right-hand drive as well as left. Larsen's circle-polished fascia is similar to that of the Aero Merlin.

Beneath the skin, the two round-tubed spaceframe chassis are quite similar visually. Neither has much obvious sign of triangulation, but the forward section of Larsen's vehicle seems to have been more effective than that of the original M3W; at any rate, there have been no reports of structural failure. One major change in the Morgan is the addition of the traditional wooden frame between the steel chassis and the aluminium panels. This does actually play a useful role.

The entire driveline and running gear are altered, however. For a start, while Larsen managed to acquire Harley-Davidson engines for his ultra-low volume operation, this was the MMC's first stumbling block.

"We talked to Harley-Davidson Europe and they were up for it; very enthusiastic," explains Mark Reeves. "But then the HD main office said ' ... no, we're a Tier One company' ... " That means that it wasn't interested in getting into low-volume supply to a specialist manufacturer.

Morgan's volumes, especially at the start, when only a run of 200 or 400 was expected, were not of interest to the USA's biggest motorcycle manufacturer. So instead, Morgan turned to the USA's second-biggest motorcycle engine manufacturer, S&S, which makes engines for Harley owners. The engine is considered in detail in chapter ten.

Those of you who have been paying attention will probably now be asking a question: if virtually nothing of the Liberty ACE made its way through into the production Morgan 3 Wheeler, why did the Morgan Motor Company buy the rights to it from Pete Larsen? It's a very good question and I am glad you asked.

In fact, there are more similarities between the Liberty ACE and the M3W than can be detected by the naked eye. On closer forensic inspection, they are very obviously close relations, with nearly identical proportions, and, of course, one can immediately see the influence of Larsen's body design and chassis construction.

The front suspension of the Morgan borrows its exact dimensions from Larsen's creation. Its uprights are constructed in a unique way to resemble the traditional sliding pillar, and the wishbones are asymmetrical. The tubular chassis is morphed from the ACE, right down to the exposed tube running along the upper part of the driver's hip.

The geometry of the Morgan's asymmetric front wishbones was not exactly scientifically conceived, and was further compromised by the use of existing spindles and knock-off hubs: these add unsprung weight and extra offset to the wheel assembly.

Pete Larsen adds: "One main item that they were buying was my concept of the remote flywheel – driven, but not supported by the engine, and a cush drive of some kind in between. All in all, I see my ideas and dimensions everywhere within the 'different' car: the DNA is 99 percent. Plus, that was their prototype ... "

Larsen is convinced that, "Morgan did not pay royalties without reason, to be sure. They reckon to have saved a year or two buying into my design, and I believe that is conservative, as most of these areas were new to them."

The MMC appeared unwilling to acknowledge publicly its debt to Pete Larsen, but now seems to have relented. There is no shame in it. As Pete says:

"Everywhere on the Morgan are ideas cribbed from the ACE: the trellis chassis from 1.5in tube, exposed to view inside; the unusual front suspension upright construction (to suggest sliding pillars); the actual wishbone dimensions and most other dimensions as well ...

"A critical idea, not self-evident to someone starting to lay out such a vehicle, is that the flywheel be supported independently of the engine crank: other small manufactures had not recognized this and abandoned similar projects.

"What they got from me was a load of ideas compressed into a hugely driveable vehicle: enough to make Charles swoon when he finally drove it, and convince all that this was something they should be doing."

A crucial player was the Niche Vehicle Network, an independent British association of over 100 niche vehicle manufacturers (among them Aston Martin, Westfield and Morgan), specialist technology companies and suppliers. From initial concept to production the M3W was supported by the NVN. This enabled the MMC to assemble in a short space of time all the pieces in its complex, three-dimensional jigsaw puzzle.

Steve Morris commented in 2011 that " ... without the support of the Niche Vehicle Network, the project would not have gone ahead at this time. Ironically, the need to invest in developing new products is crucial during economic downturn, so that they are market-ready as the economy recovers. The grant funding and support we have received has been vital in exploiting this opportunity, not just for Morgan but also for the specialist supply chain in the region."

Thus, Morgan returned to the concept of its roots after a gap of 60 years. As Matthew Welch remarks: "We had many challenges whilst developing the Morgan 3 wheeler, but also equal amounts of fun and satisfaction in creating such a unique and fun vehicle. It presented some unique challenges, not only for us here at Morgan, but also for the people who helped with testing, transportation of the cars, and even the approval authorities and registration departments." Not to mention us, the owners!

Chapter six

A big pair of pots

The Morgan 3 Wheeler may be cool, but its engine is square: both bore and stroke measure 4.25in (107.95mm). These dimensions give a capacity of 121in³ (1976cc), so each of those big cylinders has a greater swept volume than those in the Dodge/Chrysler Viper's truck-based 8.4-litre V10.

Non-bikers looking at the Morgan for the first time often ask, "Is that a Harley-Davidson engine?" There is a certain resemblance – both are big, ostentatious, shiny, air-cooled American V-twins with single-pin crankshafts, but the V-twin in the M3W differs considerably from a Harley. The most obvious external difference, one that H-D bikers notice immediately, even if they've not previously seen an S&S motor, is that the vee is considerably wider – 56 degrees instead of the 45 degrees of most vee engines, though the Moto Guzzi engine used in Trikings is 90 degrees, and other vee engines have had wider angles than that.

It was at the suggestion of Harley-Davidson, which had declined to supply engines, that the MMC turned instead to S&S Cycle, an engine tuner and manufacturer founded by George Smith and Stan Stankos in 1958. Stankos left the company and retired not long after this collaboration began, and the company then became Smith & Smith, because it was owned and run by Mr and Mrs Smith. George Smith's wife's maiden name was also Smith, so there was no need to change the logo. The headquarters of both S&S and H-D are in Wisconsin. Since 1969, S&S has been based at Viola, where the local high school is named Kickapoo. Anyway, that's history, which Henry Ford did not actually describe as bunk ... or not entirely.

S&S was the first motorcycle engine manufacturer to produce pre-certified United States Environmental Protection Agency compliant engines, lifting the burden and cost of performing the complicated EPA testing procedures from the companies and enthusiasts who buy S&S engines. The company also produces TÜV certified engines, and has even succeeded in complying with California's unique emissions requirements.

Shane Whitty of S&S explains that the X-Wedge " ... was designed specifically for OEM customers. Therefore, it was imperative that the engine not only provide great power, reliability, and ease of service, but it had to satisfy EPA, California (CARB), and even international emissions requirements.

"Today, S&S Cycle still offers the X-Wedge in a fully emissions-compliant trim. Of course, for those that plan to use the engine in a non-emissions controlled vehicle and setting (such as the race track), we also offer some very respectable performance upgrades. But again, these are not to be used in an emissions-controlled environment, such as a public highway."

The main business of S&S is supplying high-performance replacement engines and components for Harley-Davidsons, but since 2007 it has produced its own proprietary V-twin, the X-Wedge.

Originally, the standard X-Wedge, the X117 (117in³ or 1917cc) was going to be installed in the Morgan, but it was decided early on to fit the more powerful X121, which still meets emissions compliance requirements. The biggest X-Wedge, the X128 (128in³/2099cc) is now a high-cost option for M3W owners.

S&S is the second-largest motorcycle engine manufacturer in the USA, after Harley-Davidson. The Morgan contract is a small contributor to its total sales. But not the smallest of all: a version of the X-Wedge is installed in the all-new, limited-edition Hesketh 24 motorcycle introduced in 2014 – 24 because that was the number of James Hunt's Formula 1 Hesketh 308 in 1975, when he won the Dutch Grand Prix, and 24 because that is the number of 24s that Hesketh hopes to sell; possibly an ambitious total considering the eye-watering asking price, substantially above that of the Morgan 3 wheeler. If someone ever produces a powered monocycle using the X-Wedge, you can expect the price to be astronomical.

The X-Wedge range was a fresh-paper design, created especially for the custom market. It does not actually fit as a replacement engine into H-D frames, mainly because of the wider vee but also because of the motor mounting points. The wider angle was used to accommodate the layout of the three-cam design, which is made up of two exhaust cams, and one shared intake cam.

The X-Wedge was never originally intended or designed for use in any sort of car. However, as Shane Whitty of S&S explains, it " ... certainly did take advantage of the design of certain components that have been proven out in the automotive industry. For example, the one-piece forged crankshaft with two-piece, side-by-side steel connecting rods with plain bearings, as well as the automotive-style rocker arms, and even the combustion chamber design."

So far, no other car manufacturers have used the X-Wedge. That may change. "Given Morgan's success with the X-Wedge, I'm sure it's only a matter of time", says Shane Whitty.

Pete Larsen says of the X-Wedge: "It rocked the industry, but sadly the custom market was going down the tubes at the time of the introduction of the new piece. I told a BBC guy in an interview that it was dressed for the party with nowhere to go when Morgan discovered it – a truly well-met marriage in my opinion. I've got nothing but superlatives for the motor: it's a brute which is up to the task at hand, even though the Morgan is really heavier than it should be."

This S&S motor and Harley-Davidson's latest engines are more divergent than ever. While H-D has gone for harmonic balancer shafts, the X-Wedge, as well as the wider V-angle, has a number of unusual features. It has a forged, one-piece crankshaft and automotive-style plain bearings. Also in car engine style, it has low-mass rocker arms. It has a 'gerotor style' (ie generated rotor, or positive displacement) oil pump. The closed-loop fuel injection system with knock-sensing ignition is an in-house design.

Considering its large capacity, this 125in^3 version of the X-Wedge is by no means over-stressd, at least theoretically. It puts out around 115bhp and 103lbft of torque at the flywheel – that's the way car people express the figures (for bikers it's what arrives at the rear contact patch that matters). The one-piece forged crankshaft, incidentally, adds around 3kg to the overall weight of the engine, but it reduces vibrations.

Note that the verb is 'reduces.' If you seek V12 smoothness, look elsewhere. The lumpiness in the running of a V-twin of this type is easily explained. There is combustion in cylinder A, then in cylinder B 315 degrees later; then there is a 405-degree hiatus before Cylinder A fires, then 315, then 405 and so on. Potato, potato, potato ...

Harley-Davidson had many quality problems in the past, and

Around 240 people are employed by S&S to make the X-Wedge possible, but final assembly is carried out by only six skilled workers. (Courtesy S&S)

To left and right centre are the inlet camshaft pulleys, top centre is the exhaust camshaft pulley, and at the bottom is the crankshaft pulley. (Courtesy S&S)

went through an especially rough patch in the 1990s. In particular, its engines were prone to leak oil, though some H-D aficionados, suffering perhaps from an automotive form of Stockholm Syndrome (which also afflicts a number of Morgan 3 Wheeler owners) insisted they did not leak, they merely " ... marked their spot." H-D's motors have improved considerably in recent years, partly by copying some of the features introduced by S&S.

However, it's important to remember that the Harley motor is mass-produced. S&S began by offering re-engineered Harley engines. They just made them differently – and much more expensive, machined from billet and far stronger, essential because of the larger capacities.

The pushrod S&S V-twin is the first power plant of its type to meet EPA 2010 US Tier II standards in all 49 North American states. It might be described as 'eco-friendly,' though only up to a point: if you fire it up before dawn your neighbours may have other words for it ... and for you.

Recommended fuel for this engine is top-end 98-Octane. This arrives from the twin rear tanks (total capacity 42 litres) in each of those big combustion chambers thanks to CLEFI (Closed Loop Electronic Fuel Injection), which delivers the air/fuel mixture in precise proportions through a single 2in-diameter inlet valve. Compressed and burned, the gas then exits via a 1.605in exhaust valve, passing via a catalytic converter towards the atmosphere. There is no four-valve head for the X-Wedge, but Whitty says: "Again, for racing and other off-highway, non-emissions controlled applications, we do offer a CNC ported head with even larger valves for higher performance."

At the front of the engine as fitted in the M3W there is a shiny, triangular cover plate (actually an irregular heptagon). Behind this is the timing gear. The lowest pulley is attached to the end of the crankshaft, and this drives the camshafts via a toothed belt. If the belt snaps for one reason or another, there's little chance of major damage away from the local area, because the motor is of a 'non-interference' design, which means that the valves and pistons cannot collide with each other.

With CLEFI and the catalyst (which sounds like a 1960s pop group), one might expect slightly lower emissions than the rated 215g/km, which is more, for example, than is put out by the far higher-performing Porsche Boxster S, probably the penalty of that non-interference design, in which the combustion chambers are inevitably less efficient than they might be.

The X-Wedge has been widely praised in the motorcycling press. 'Sir' Alan Cathcart, one of the world's leading motorbike journalists, wrote in *Motorcyclist* magazine: "Despite lacking a counter-balancer, the 95-horsepower X-Wedge motor is satisfactorily smooth all the way across the rev range. It's very refined in terms of operation, too, starting, idling and injecting without any issues to speak of."

As well as those qualities, the X-Wedge has a reputation for being strong and reliable, if not actually bomb-proof, provided it is carefully run-in according to the company's strict rules. However, there have been a few failures, mostly behind the timing belt casing at the bottom end of the front of the engine.

The X-Wedge's timing is by toothed belt, which is often a worry because of the 'Apocalypse Now' scenario that can swiftly follow the failure of the belt.

However, in this engine, as already explained, such a failure is generally not the prelude to disaster. A number of Morgan 3 Wheeler owners, myself included, have good reason to be relieved that this feature is part of the design.

Some belts in M3Ws have failed on their own, without provocation, for no obvious reason. It has been suggested that heat can be a factor, and the latest version of the standard engine at the time of writing has shims between the timing case cover and the crankcase to allow hot air to escape. Moto Guzzi engines have had a ventilated spacer for years to reduce the build-up of heat in the alternator.

Sometimes the belt doesn't fail of its own accord. The long, tapered bolt that holds the crankcase sprocket in place has a vexing tendency to come loose, and it then flies forward, punching through the shiny aluminium alloy casing – and, of course, ripping the belt to shreds and bringing silence where there had been a high dBA output.

Heat was certainly not a factor when this happened to me, and I had never been stuck in traffic during the 2745km that I had covered since taking delivery. My engine had never switched itself into 'Skip Fire Mode.' I had carefully observed the running-in regime. I had never 'lugged' my motor, and even when I had run it in, I rarely used more than 5000rpm, because there's not much point. One careful owner ...

I was heading west early on a sunny but surprisingly cold morning in May 2014, cruising along what is now called the D75 (actually the old RN75, France's most famous Route Nationale, equivalent, perhaps, to the USA's old Route 66) at around the speed limit of 90kph, when suddenly there was a total loss of power. There was no seizure and no audible graunching of metal components. It just stopped, and then there was silence. Unfortunately, it stopped on an incline and the nearest safe place was about 50 yards ahead; so I had to push. I am not 20 any more, but somehow I managed it, while huge articulated freight transport whistled past. Eventually, after a couple of pauses for breath, I reached the sanctuary, the entry to a vineyard. I went to the front to check if there was anything obvious that had gone wrong, and indeed there was: a hole had been punched through the lower part of timing cover, and the crankshaft pulley retaining bolt was visible.

In August 2014, I was informed that S&S was " ... trying currently to understand why this happens." But at the time of going to press it remained a mystery no longer wrapped in a timing case. Moto Guzzi had encountered a similar problem a few years ago, on its new four-valve engine. It seems the first batch had an incorrect washer fitted. There have been no problems since.

One mystery to me concerning this problem is that the bolt is not engineered to turn against the direction of rotation, which I thought was basic engineering practice. Another is that S&S specifically forbids the use of adhesives (even one of the milder blue types), such as Loctite, to hold it in place.

If the timing belt fails in the X-Wedge, the engine will not destroy itself: there cannot be contact between valves and pistons. (Courtesy Nigel Smith)

Chapter seven

The driveline – a game of consequences

Having failed to secure the supply of engines from Harley-Davidson and Moto Guzzi, as detailed earlier, the MMC then took the project forward with S&S. This had dramatic consequences for the driveline, which led to development delays (the delays were not sufficiently extended, some might say) and warranty problems, especially for the first year's production.

When you read that an engine has peak torque of such and such a figure, you may imagine (as I used to) that that is the maximum output of the engine. However, it is only a nominal figure, and there can be spikes of torque considerably higher than that supposed maximum. In the case of the X-Wedge, these can be stupefyingly massive, multiplying that nominal figure at the flywheel by a factor of 10 or even 15. It is no wonder that this motor caused some difficulties further down the line in the M3W ... The trouble is, torque eats the heart out of transmissions. As Andrew English wrote in *The Daily Telegraph*:

"S&S says [the X-Wedge] produces torque spikes of 1800lb/ft, which makes the gears clash and sing against each other. [Mark] Reeves and his team, together with S&S, have adapted a Harley-Davidson mechanical cushion drive, which successfully irons out the firing impulses. The engine sits on a rubber-mounted bed plate, and the stainless steel exhausts have flexible couplings and mountings. Start her up and you see a lot of movement, but the cabin and major controls are stock still."

At that stage the adverb 'successfully' was employed optimistically by the MMC. Since then, the installation of the Centa coupling and other changes further down the driveline have greatly reduced the capacity for havoc of the violent V-twin of Wisconsin.

Early on, the five-speed Mazda gearbox from the MX-5/Miata was selected. This was probably the best choice available, because of its excellent reputation for robustness. Though it is not actually based on the original MX-5 gearbox, which had originally been designed for use in the B2000/B2200 pickup, it seems to be made of the right stuff. It has a satisfactory torque rating, which is just as well in this application, as you will have gathered. It has a good reputation for reliability in the M3W, having remained intact while components either side of it have expired. The only failure I have heard of occurred when someone allowed his 3 Wheeler to be towed, which is specifically prohibited.

The standard Mazda dry-plate clutch is also used, and there seem to have been no problems with it. It could problem cope with an increase in engine output, but there are heavier-duty competition versions available if necessary.

As well as being tough, this gearbox has an excellent gear-change, which has been widely praised in road tests. The only minor criticism that could be made is that reverse is slightly obstructive.

As for the ratios, they are fine in normal use, but not perfect in a couple of respects. One of these is practical: first gear seems unnecessarily low, though one would not wish to raise it too much. The second minor flaw is more a public relations issue. Zero to 60mph are a bit of a nonsense in the real world, but they are good for getting headlines. Now, supposing you want to get the best possible 0-60mph time, you definitely do not want to have to change gear twice below that speed.

With the final drive of 4.13:1, maximum speeds in the first four gears are 32, 53, 75 and 100mph, with a theoretical 122mph in fifth. A higher-volume manufacturer than Morgan would undoubtedly adjust the internal ratios to allow second gear to exceed 60mph. That's not an option, so the only alternative would be to alter the final drive ratio. If it were numerically lowered to 3.6:1, that would give speeds in the lower

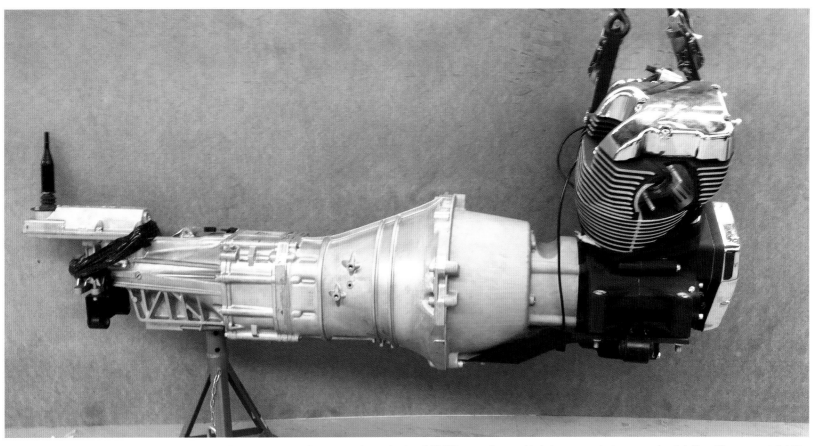

S&S engine and Mazda gearbox, ready for installation. Between them is the CENTA coupling, which has greatly improved reliability. (Courtesy MMC)

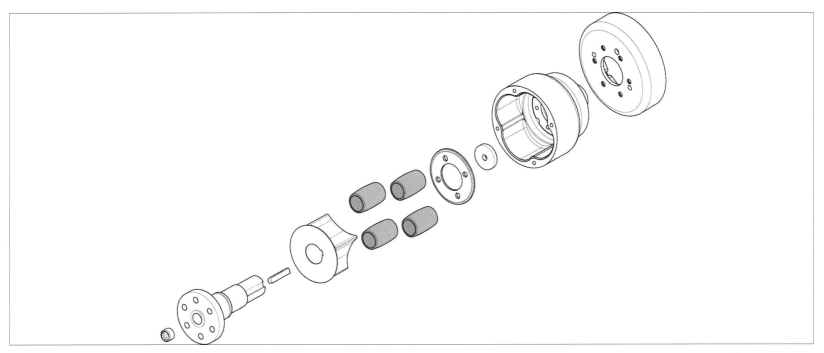

Exploded view of the CENTA coupling, which helps to mollify the violent torque pulses from the big V-twin. (Courtesy MMC)

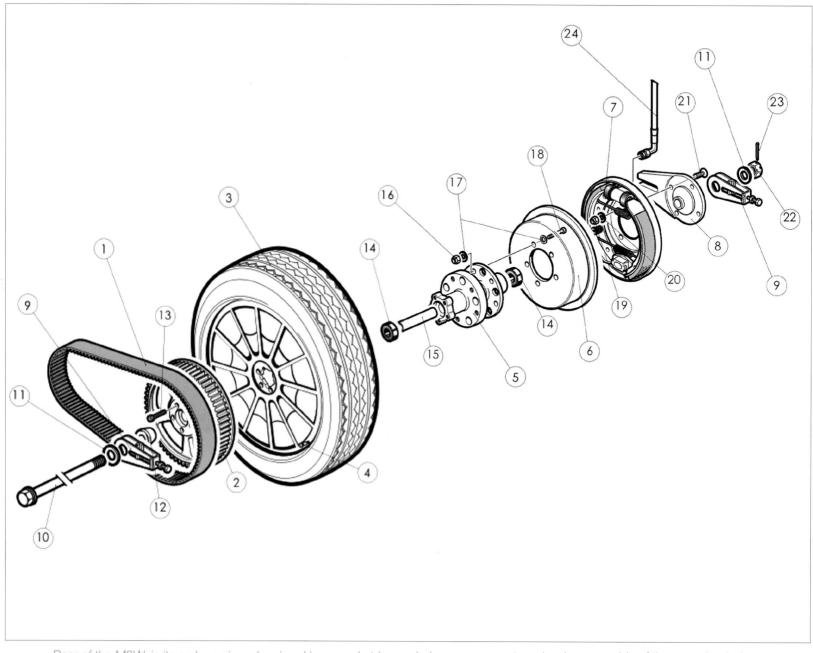

Rear of the M3W, in its early version, showing drive sprocket (upgraded on more recent versions) on one side of the rear wheel; drum brake on the other. (Courtesy MMC)

gears of 37, 60.784, 86 and 115mph, with a theoretical 141mph in fifth. To attain 100kph (62.2mph) in second, an even greater numerical reduction would be required.

This high fifth would perhaps not be too bad, because at 120mph, you would be running at just below 5000rpm. However, if the M3W could actually exceed 115mph with this gearing, which is possible (probably in fourth), front tyres with a higher speed rating would be required.

There are other 19in tyres with a higher speed rating, but not with a flattish profile, better to go down to 18in, then the world is your oyster.

It is either side of this gearbox that problems have arisen. Although the S&S motor has a reputation for being strong and reliable (though the timing belt problems outlined in the previous chapter have somewhat dented that), it is not actually as smooth as a Harley because, as previously mentioned, it does not have harmonic

Changing a rear tyre is more complex than on normal cars, or on the Liberty ACE with its single swinging rear arm.

balancers. Even the tough Mazda gearbox would have been given a hammering if attached directly, so that was not an option.

"Because it requires an oil bath and is oriented incorrectly for shaft-drive, among other reasons, I dismissed the 'compensator' as an option for the ACE. Morgan fell back on the compensator against my counsel, and indeed the reworked compensators proved unsuitable." Pete Larsen adds:

"Morgan at first did not understand the significance or need for such a component, but then began to work on their own version of my design. Their prototype had a fatal flaw, failed, and was abandoned in favour of re-worked Harley pieces ... the notorious 'compensator.' I'm certain this was done at the suggestion of S&S who would be familiar with it from motorcycle applications. Morgan has come to regret this choice, and the 'Frankenstein' design: the new CENTA is an elastomeric coupling, as was mine, worlds apart in durability, silence and simplicity."

Matthew Welch adds: "I wish we had found the current design of CENTA centre drive between the engine and flywheel at the start. We spent a lot of time trying different designs on this, and had we discovered CENTA and their coupling earlier we would have had much more time to spend testing and improving the car, and would've avoided some of the early issues we had with things like the cracking chassis and exhausts."

Chapter eight

Body/frame/chassis/suspension

The woodiness of Morgans is, perhaps, the main feature that attracts people's interest. The 3 Wheeler has a pronounced diuretic effect. I was just about to climb back into the beast after stopping in an aire on a French Route Nationale when a lorry driver jumped out of his cab and ran over. He asked politely if he could take a photograph, and then said, "Le chassis est en bois, n'est-ce pas?" "Not exactly," I replied, trying to remember the French for 'frame.' I'm still not sure ... 'cadre,' I think. Well, the easiest way round the problem was to show him where the ash frame is between the steel chassis tubes and the aluminium panels. He was fascinated by this survivor from the olden days of coachbuilding. I did not have sufficient time to remove the fibre insert in the luggage compartment and show him that section, which is the most interesting part.

A completed 3 Wheeler ash frame is a beautiful object, one that would look good suspended from a high ceiling. I'd rather have one of those in my house than a sectioned shark in aspic. The pieces of the ash frame are cut and shaped using labour-intensive methods, and tooling that would have been familiar not only to Malvern's Morgan workers more than a century ago, but also to 19th century coachbuilders, when the coaches were drawn by our four-legged friends. They are chemically treated, so worry not – your ash frame will not be attacked by weevils or dry rot, certainly not in the first decade or two of ownership. Morgan, incidentally, has sufficient supplies of ash for production until 2020.

A great deal of expert hand finishing is necessary for the frame, requiring a high degree of accuracy because, when batches of completed frames arrive at the Premier Group's factory in Coventry, they are fitted with the aluminium body panels designed and manufactured with computerized precision.

A batch of these completed frames is dispatched by lorry to

Premier, whose current motor industry clients include Jaguar Land Rover, Ford and Bentley, and in other industries Alstom, GKN, JCB, Bombardier and Dyson. In the past, Premier has worked with Rolls-Royce, Ricardo, Johnson Controls, and ItalDesign. A major contract was the manufacture of 11,000 torches for the 2012 London Olympics.

Premier first started working with Morgan in 2008. The first contract was for two components used in the Morgan classic range. Then the bodyshells of the Aeromax and the Supersport limited editions (about 120 of each) were made.

For the M3W, Premier manufactures the complete body-in-white (including the front lid, the boot and the cockpit), and it also manufactures the front mudguards and the twin fuel tanks.

The completed frames and bodies are then transferred back to Malvern to be painted (by a worker with a spray gun rather than a spooky robot) and finished, and then introduced to the steel chassis. This is made by ABT of Ross-on-Wye, Herefordshire, using round tubes from Top Tubes Ltd of Wednesbury, between Wolverhampton and Birmingham. Like Premier, both these companies have clients in a wide range of industries.

ABT has manufactured chassis for a variety of vehicles, including sports cars, grass cutting machines, earth movers, specialist military vehicles, hybrid electric vehicles, and crop sprayers. It manufactures all the steel classic chassis for Morgan, and some small ancillaries, such as gearbox mounts and frame fronts. Jaguar and Land Rover are among its other clients. Top Tubes is a supplier to Ford, Porsche, Maserati, Jaguar, Rolls Royce, Vauxhall and Volvo. The first prototype chassis was completed at the end of 2010, and production began in March 2011.

The first chassis were made from S235 steel tube, Ø38.1mm/2mm

The ash frame of the M3W performs a useful structural function, but is also a thing of beauty. (Courtesy Blake Marvin/MMC)

Although hand-made by traditional methods, the frame must also be highly accurate in its measurements: Premier's aluminium panels are manufactured with computerised precision. (Courtesy MMC)

On its return to Pickersleigh Road after a trip to Coventry, a frame, now married to the body panels, awaits preparation, painting and introduction to the chassis. (Courtesy MMC)

thick, but, explains Mark Edge of ABT: "After some chassis failures due to metal fatigue, it was changed to ERW S355 Ø38.1mm (outside diameter)/2.03mm thick. At this time we also added support gussets to the engine bay tubes to increase strength. In November 2013 we introduced the latest design upgrade with triangulation engine bay support tubes which replaced the previously fitted brace bar configuration."

All the information available suggests that it was only the earliest 2012 versions that were prone to cracking, and many of those have

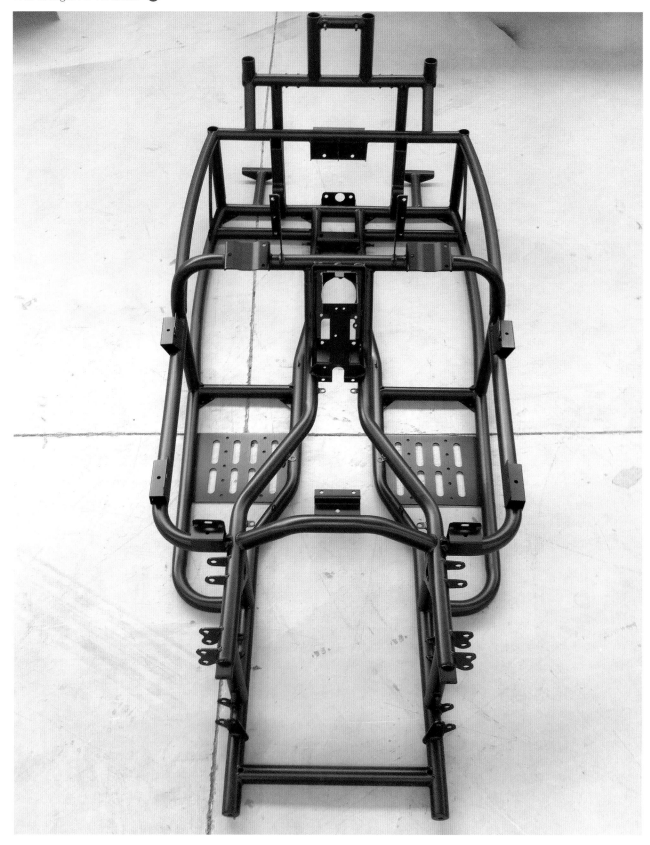

A 2014 chassis – considerably more rigid than its predecessors. (Courtesy MMC)

Okay chaps, for your next test, try that with the engine and gearbox installed ... Marc Cerrone (foreground) and a colleague place a chassis on trestles for the start of assembly. (Courtesy MMC)

had their chassis replaced. If you are considering buying one of those, check the paperwork carefully.

The manufacture of a 3 Wheeler chassis from start to finish takes approximately 18 hours. Processes involved include laser cutting, press brake folding of various parts, tube bending operations, machining and drilling holes, pressing (end of tube preparation for joints), welding, autophoretic (AP) coating, which is rust protection of internal and external surfaces, and finally the top coat spray. ABT also manufactures the front wishbones, the rear trailing arms, and the bevel box mounts for the M3W.

And now we return to Pickersleigh Road ...

After the engine and gearbox, in goes the steering rack. (Courtesy MMC)

Although the majority of work on the M3W in the factory, apart from woodwork and leather trim, is assembly rather than construction, it remains a labour-intensive process. (Courtesy MMC)

Chapter nine

How it is put together

Morgans in the past were genuinely hand-built. To a large extent, almost all the fabrication, including the chassis and body panels, took place inside the factory, though the company has always bought in most of the mechanical components. It has never manufactured its own engines, which may be one of the keys to its longevity (certainly one of the major factors in the demise of TVR was the ambitious decision to follow the opposite path).

These days, although there's still a lot of traditional craftsmanship to be found in Pickersleigh Road, the emphasis, as already noted, has switched more to hand assembly, especially with regard to the M3W. This is an important distinction, and a major shift towards the methods advised by Sir John Harvey-Jones.

However, as detailed in the previous chapter, not only the chassis and the body of the M3W, but almost everything else, is supplied in completed or nearly-completed form by sub-contractors.

In the early days, the entire assembly process was contracted out to Vitesse, in Hinckley, but when it became clear that the initial estimates of demand were seriously low, and that demand was booming, MMC brought the project back in-house.

Construction of a 3 Wheeler, as detailed in the previous chapter, begins with the ash frame. Toward the end of the production journey, the other remaining craft work area is the leather trim – for the seats, armrests, transmission tunnel, outer parts of the dashboard, and the little tags that protect the paint of the beetle back from the Dzus fasteners. With foam padding in places, this is cut and stitched and glued where necessary, the hides having arrived from Andrew Muirhead of Glasgow, Scotland.

Apart from the wood and leather, the major work on the M3W carried out inside the factory is assembly. Other than that and the spraying of paint, almost everything else before final testing and

delivery happens elsewhere. As Mark Reeves explains: "In the factory we assemble the Centa drive and join the engine and transmission together. We assemble the front hubs, disks, etc onto the uprights. We also assemble the rear hub, drum, etc. That's about it!"

Batches of framed bodies arrive from Premier to the MMC where they are painted. Meanwhile, a batch of chassis arrives from ABT Products of Ross-on-Wye. The engine, transmission and suspension are attached, and then the frame/body goes on.

When a bare chassis is taken off the rack at Malvern, before it is introduced to the body/frame, it is placed on a stout pair of old-fashioned wooden trestles, to be fitted with the suspension and wheels. Standard springs and dampers, as already mentioned, are from Spax, but there are also upgraded sets from both Spax and Suplex which will be fitted at this stage if specified.

Standard front tyres are from Avon, on wire wheels (off-the-shelf items designed for the 1936-1939 MG TA) made by Motor Wheel Service International of Slough, while several different makes of rear tyre have been used. The rear wheel is from Rimstock of West Bromwich, " ... the world's leading manufacturer of alloy wheels."

The various elements of the driveline are fitted. Starting at the rear wheel in the reverse direction of drive, these begin with a motorcycle-

Opposite, top: A considerable amount of preparation and finishing is necessary in the paint shop. (Courtesy Blake Marvin/MMC)

Opposite, left: Bending the tubes: the early stage of chassis construction at ABT Products. (Courtesy ABT)

A Morgan 3 Wheeler chassis being welded on the jig at ABT. (Courtesy ABT)

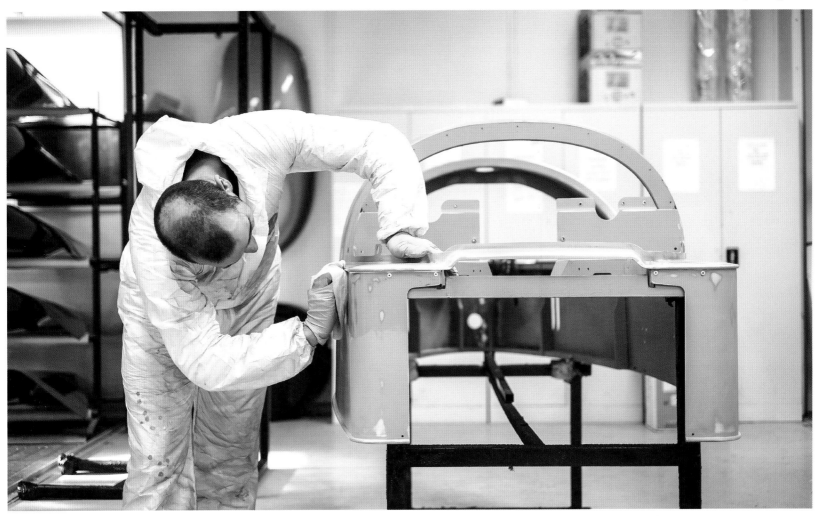

Four M3W chassis set off from the ABT factory toward Malvern with a batch of galvanized chassis for the 'trads.' (Courtesy ABT)

type wheel bearing and an aluminium drive sprocket from Quaife. This is connected to the bevel box sprocket by a toothed carbon fibre belt made by the Scottish division of Gates, a global corporation based in Denver, Colorado, USA.

The Morgan's bevel box is made by Quaife. Next item upstream is a short cardan shaft, which comes off the back end of the Mazda five-speed gearbox, and a standard dry-plate clutch assembly (shipped from Hiroshima). Separating the gearbox bellhousing from the engine is the CENTA coupling, standard fitting since early 2014 (before that there were two generations of a compensator created by the MMC and S&S, the second of which was slightly less troublesome than the first).

The steering rack, another Quaife product, goes on, with the steering column supplied by Franco-British specialist Traven. The steering wheel is from Moto Lita (which makes some nicer wheels at higher prices). The entire braking system – master cylinder, front discs and callipers, rear drum, servo – is supplied by Caparo, which gives

Two chassis await the works treatment. They may never meet again.
(Courtesy MMC)

A Quaife bevel box, silently awaiting installation in a Morgan 3 Wheeler. (Courtesy MMC)

A line-up of front hubs ready to join the action. (Courtesy Blake Marvin/MMC)

The bevel box, as installed. Access to it requires removal of numerous panels. (Courtesy Graham Sherwood)

the M3W a vague Indian connection, though all the parts are made in Britain.

Next, the S&S engine, having arrived in a batch from Wisconsin, is bolted in place. The exhaust system, including the heat shields, is supplied by Janspeed of Salisbury, Wiltshire. The 3 Wheeler's wiring loom and electrical system, from Raffenday of Wellingborough, Northants, is installed. Headlamps and sidelights come from Maxparts of Farnborough, Hants, and the instruments from VDO (and the speedo is not its fault!), now part of the Continental AG group. Rear-view mirrors are by Lacey.

The ultra-light fibre boot insert is from Sparlonz of Redditch, Worcestershire. This company specialises in vacuum forming and thermoforming, and this is a well-made component: do not blame the company for the leaks. The cowl badge and the aero screens are supplied by MAP.

The M3W's fuse box is well placed under the front cowl, and is easy to understand thanks to the identification key on the inside of the lid.

FINAL FINISH BAY 4

Stitching in the leather shop – another craft skill that continues in the factory. (Courtesy Blake Marvin/MMC)

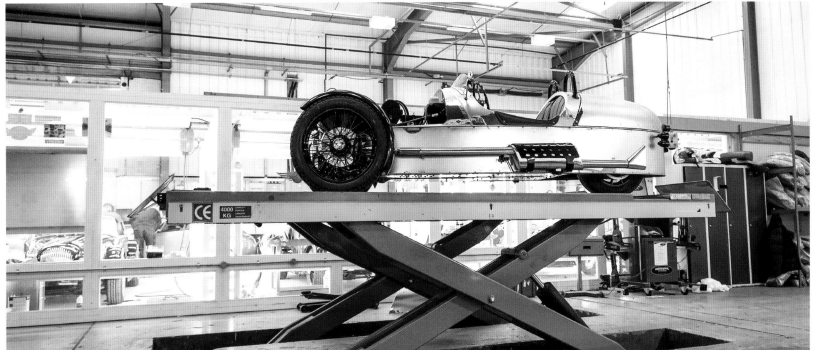

Apart from the seats and armrests, leftover strips of leather are used for the rear cowl tags, and to provide protection between aluminium panels. (Courtesy Blake Marvin/MMC)

Final inspection. The Pickersleigh Road factory is a much lighter place than when Sir John Harvey-Jones visited. (Courtesy Blake Marvin/MMC)

Stamped on the plate is the build number (931), and on the body panel, Premier's number (882). 'MOO-1,' the paint code, is for black, not brown.

A very shiny M3W with Brooklands steering wheel and exhaust awaits collection/dispatch. (Courtesy Blake Marvin/MMC)

Chapter ten

My first drive

I n this chapter, I shall describe my first impressions of driving the M3W. In the following chapter, you'll be able to read a more detailed evaluation of the machine, with my revised opinions after I had run it in and could push it harder.

My first drive was a fairly tiring experience, but not exactly a baptism of fire. For one thing, there was intermittent rain on my long journey – 360 miles/600km – from the dealer on the outskirts of Toulouse to my house in the Var.

This is confession time: I had committed the fundamental 'no-no' of car buying – ordering without first going for a test drive. In fact, I had never previously seen a 3 Wheeler close up before that morning at Marcassus when I took delivery. Well, His Holiness may float around on his cloud of infallibility, but even cardinals make errors, so what chance is there for the rest of us mere mortals? I was relieved to find that I did actually fit into the machine and could operate the pedals without too much difficulty.

It was less uncomfortable than I had expected, but the first mental note I made was to obtain a spacer to bring the steering wheel closer, because my left knee, my left hand, and the steering wheel were all in conflict with each other. I have since discovered that this is less of a problem with right-hand drive models, because the relatively low transmission tunnel allows the clutch leg to bend more easily than in my car, where the body/chassis gets in the way, and, of course, the right leg is applying the throttle so is not as bent.

My second observation was that, while I had previously considered the steering lock of my 2011 Honda Civic to be appallingly bad, this device set new standards in this respect. The third was that at parking speed, the steering was also very heavy.

I buckled up, depressed the clutch, flicked up the cover on the slightly silly 'Bombs Away' device in the centre of the dash, and pressed START. Gosh, that's loud!

I inserted earplugs, put on helmet and gloves, thought, "I must be totally barmy," and set off for home, soon finding with relief that required steering effort was greatly reduced once one got above parking speed, though it is still by no means light in comparison with modern cars; even those without power assistance. Also, it tracks straight and true on a smooth surface, and the feel, pre 'Comfort Kit' (of which more later) is admirably fine, especially around the straight-ahead position, where most modern cars, even including some generally good driving machines, are mildly fuzzy.

The first downpour occurred about an hour into my journey. I was lucky. I was in slow-moving traffic on the edge of a town and, just as the rain was beginning to be uncomfortable, I saw a structure like a series of carports conveniently at the side of the road. It was a jet-wash centre, which of course was not being used that day, there being no obviously mad people around, apart from me.

I drove in and was comfortably sheltered while I got out, stretched my legs and put on the waterproof coat (actually more like the upper half of a frogman's outfit) I had bought specially for the trip. Then I took it off again, because the rain stopped. I had a 'slash' at the rear of the premises and then headed east again.

The M3W has already covered 50 miles/80km and has had an initial oil change when delivered to your dealer. After that, it's very important to follow the running-in instructions, which is simultaneously boring and quite demanding.

S&S recommends in its handbook for motorcycle users of this engine that " ... for the next 500 miles [after that initial oil change] try to keep the rpm below 4000. Avoid lugging the engine or maintaining a constant rpm level for any appreciable time. Lugging the motor would be low rpm in a high gear; this is never good on your V-twin motor. Always try to be above 2700 at all times while the bike is moving down the highway. Change the oil and filter at 500 miles/800km. From 500 to 1000 miles/1600km, ride the motorcycle normally, but be conservative with the harsh treatments. Avoid racing, burnouts or dyno runs."

My dealer advised an even more cautious regime than this, keeping between 2700 and 3500rpm until the first service at 1000 miles, and so I did.

To an extent, this was fine for cruising on French A-roads, where the speed limit is 90kph (56mph), though I was constantly changing gears and altering my speed slightly, as it is well known that new engines should not simply be kept at constant revs. Fortunately, the gear-change was as crisp as I remembered it from driving Mazda MX-5s, though this one is the next generation of those I had used.

The greatest surprise early on was that ride comfort was not too bad most of the time. I had expected it to be rock solid and jarring, but actually, provided you take care to avoid the more severe bumps and pot-holes, it is reasonably supple and absorbent.

I was obliged to take a detour because of roadworks at one point, and we were directed through a trading estate with some very rough patches. The difficulty of avoiding all the worst bits is, of course, far greater when you have a rear wheel dead centre between the path followed by the front wheels. At very low speed crossing an unavoidable dip, I noted that the track rod made contact with the exhaust – which is something to watch out for.

Then, at higher speeds, I felt that the bump steer issue, of which I had heard so much, was not quite as bad as I had feared. But this was before I had driven the beast, rather than merely cruised it. Even at this early stage, however, I was astonished that some people on the TalkMorgan website either denied that it existed or stated that it should not be a cause for complaint, because it was part of the 'character' of the vehicle.

It took me a longer time to feel sufficiently confident to push the M3W really hard on winding roads than has been the case with any other car that I've ever driven. And it is a car. Its behaviour is like that of a car, not at all comparable with a motorbike or combination. Partly of course, the long period of acclimatization is because you feel so vulnerable in this tiny little machine, and in this sense it is like a motorbike: to get the best out of it you must suspend your imagination.

I had thought that the understeer I was experiencing was merely an effect of running at low rpm, and that once I was able to extend the engine further up its range, it would be relatively easy to drive around with controlled tail slides, to steer on the throttle. The problem proved to be rather more complex than I had expected, as will be explained in the following chapter.

It was hard to be sure on the low-rev regime, but I felt even then that Morgan's performance claims were somewhat optimistic. Early in the life of the new M3W, its manufacturer suggested that it would do 0-60mph in 4.5 seconds. It was soon evident to anyone with any testing experience that this was wildly optimistic, though a large number of people writing road tests in various publications repeated this, parrot fashion. Again, more about this in the next chapter.

The worst bit about my drive home was the last couple of hours. The sun was setting, the sky was cloudless, and I decided to chop off some time by taking the A8 autoroute from Aix to Le Muy, rather than following the old RN7, which is now downgraded from a route nationale and called the DN7 under one of those strange French administrative amendments. My decision soon proved to be an error, though. I stopped at a service station, filled up with fuel, emptied my own tank, and I could see that the weather was on the turn. To be on the safe side, I put on my waterproof gear, which turned out to be a wise decision.

Soon the rain started to fall and it was also getting dark. I was struggling along, maintaining around 100-110kph (60-70mph) and I did not feel keen on going much faster anyway because of the unpleasant visibility problems. It is possibly better for shorter drivers who look through the little aero screen rather than over it, especially if they treat the screen with that water-dispersant stuff.

I found myself in a convoy of articulated lorries driven by homicidal tailgaters. I eased onto the hard shoulder, slowed to 50mph/80kph and let them get away. And then the next gang of semi-trailer lunatics arrived. I resolved to get off at the next exit and rejoin the RN7. Alas, the next exit turned out to be more than half an hour away.

During my journey, I discovered that the 3 Wheeler attracts a lot of attention. Guys on big, powerful motorbikes seem to love it, and lots of people wave or flash their headlights.

I stopped in one aire on a route nationale and emptied my bladder in the woods. I was just about to climb back aboard when a French lorry driver hopped out of his cab and came running over. He asked politely if he could take some photos, and I said yes, of course. He then said, it has a chassis made of wood, doesn't it? Well, he was not far off, and he was fascinated when I showed him how the ash frame fits between the steel chassis and the aluminium panels.

During a sunny spell, when I was cruising along a dual carriageway at around 60mph/100kph, a Porsche Cayenne pulled alongside. Both windows on my side were open and a pair of teenagers, one in front and one behind were leaning out, filming me. I felt more than ever convinced that Morgan had made a good decision in putting the M3W into production, though whether I had made a good decision in buying one is another matter.

I finally got home in one piece, without even getting thoroughly soaked. I had a large shot of Aberlour and thought, I may be a bit barmy, but that's not such a bad thing ...

The essential act on reaching home from your first drive is Woollarding. William Woollard, former presenter of Top Gear, then a serious British television programme about motoring, invented the practice.

Chapter eleven

The road test, with stars

In this chapter, I present a full road test of the Morgan 3 Wheeler, written more or less as if for a specialist motoring magazine. I have omitted from this section a full description of the vehicle, as that has been covered in previous chapters. There is analysis of how it fits into the market, and an assessment of its strengths and weaknesses.

All of this is seasoned with asides based on personal experience and knowledge, where appropriate, plus remarks on the M3W's development since its introduction in 2012. Most magazine road tests are written after between one and several drivers have been behind the wheel of a car for a few days, and many areas are not covered in great depth. I hope that here I have achieved that depth without sinking into verbosity.

I have adopted the star system we used years ago on the late lamented *Motor* (then Britain's highest-circulation weekly motoring magazine): one star for Poor, five for Excellent. Unusually, I have put the stars at the end of each section so if you wish you may read my assessments and then be surprised at the generosity or otherwise of the stars awarded.

There will be only passing reference to reliability issues, as these are covered in greater depth elsewhere.

How does the M3W fit into the market? It's a simple question but the answer is rather complex. It has featured in comparison tests with the least powerful Caterham 7, the 160, which is powered by a three-cylinder, 660cc Suzuki engine, so its swept volume is only 33 percent of the Morgan's; however, it is turbocharged. Also, at 1090lb/490kg, the Caterham has a significant weight advantage.

It may be argued that the Caterham is not a direct rival, and, indeed, that the Morgan has no real rivals, but that is a blinkered view. Each of these minimalist offerings appeals to someone who has some spare cash and who is looking for something not particularly practical in which to have fun.

There certainly is a shortage of competition from elsewhere. There are other three-wheelers from small specialist builders, such as those mentioned earlier, but one of the perceived attractions of the M3W is that it comes from a well-established, reasonably-sized company with a dealer network, so that one will receive full back-up in the event of unfortunate problems. Well, that's the theory, at least.

On this basis, the Caterham fits the bill, probably better than anything, though in some ways the most similar car in concept to the M3W that I have driven was the Light Car Company's Rocket, created in the 1990s by one of the finest racing drivers you have possibly never heard of, Chris Craft (nothing to do with the boats), and engineered by Gordon Murray. The latter had produced world championship-winning Grand Prix cars for Brabham and McLaren, and was also responsible for the McLaren F1, which, for a while, had the highest top speed (240mph/386kph) of any road car.

The Rocket was a tandem two-seater, loosely based visually on Cooper-Climax Grand Prix cars of the late 1950s, and powered by a mid-mounted 1070cc Yamaha engine, with a rather annoyingly complex transmission. It was simultaneously retro and modern. It was ultra-light, far lighter than the Morgan, but nevertheless a bit heavier in production form than had been hoped by its creators. However, funnily enough, it really did do 0-60mph in 4.4 seconds; I know, because I did the figures at Millbrook.

Two-up it was less comfortable than the M3W, but for a solo driver it was better, with space to rest the clutch foot. It was totally impractical, with no weather protection whatsoever, and zero luggage space, too, but it was huge fun, with a surprisingly comfortable ride. There was not a lot of grip; intentionally: the handling was very precise but you had to keep your wits about you. It was very much like driving a Formula Ford on the road. It was even more over-priced than the M3W, and not many were made.

Incidentally, when Gordon was designing the F1, a journalist asked him if it was his answer to Ferrari's F40. He replied acidly, "No. I don't think we have anyone at McLaren who can weld that badly." I have sometimes wondered what sort of waspish remark he would come out with if he took a look at the geometry of the M3W's front suspension.

But back to Morgan versus Caterham ... The straight-line performance of the M3W and the Caterham 160 is quite similar, the Caterham being probably a shade quicker from zero to 60mph, and the Morgan, with its higher top speed, catching and passing it thereafter. Throw in some bends and the Caterham is undoubtedly superior. In the hands of the competent and superbly-named Henry Catchpole of *EVO* magazine, the little four-wheeler was 2.3 seconds faster than the Morgan around the 1.35-mile Mallory Park circuit in Leicestershire, which is a substantial margin. So the contest is not like that between a Morgan Aero Sport versus an Austin 7 Ulster in the late 1920s.

Also, let's not forget that the Caterham 160, even fully-built by the factory rather than supplied as a kit, is substantially less expensive. For the same money as the Morgan, you could have the far more rapid Caterham 7 Supersport, or even the Supersport R, though they would be more expensive to insure.

This shows that if you want to buy a M3W you have to have a particular reason, and that reason will not be outright performance but rather the fact that it is so much a trip back to basics (and, alas, beyond at times). It starts becoming interesting, engaging and indeed quite difficult, at relatively low speeds. It is not intended as a trackday vehicle, and if an Ariel Atom is your dream machine, the M3W probably will not be, though you could have both, to suit widely different moods.

My car left the factory as build/VIN number 931 in September 2013. The chassis number is 825, the body number 882, and the ash frame number 942 (if you have a Morgan whose four identification numbers match, you win a prize). My assessments are based largely upon it, with reference here and there to its place in the evolution between 2012 and 2014 models.

PERFORMANCE

Early in the life of the new M3W, its manufacturer suggested that it would do 0-60mph in 4.5 seconds. It's not clear why this figure was snapped out of thin air. It was soon evident to anyone with any testing experience that such a time was fanciful, indeed utterly impossible, though a large number of gullible people writing road tests in various publications repeated this canard, parrot fashion (to mix avian terms), and one or two dealers had not bothered to amend it in 2014, no doubt though lack of attention ...

Morgan later revised its estimate to 0-62mph (100kph) in 6.0 seconds, which would give 0-60mph in about 5.7 seconds. This is still very much towards the pipe-dreaming end of the spectrum, though somewhat closer to reality.

If you're expecting to out-drag superbikes, supercars, or even rapid sports cars such as the Porsche Boxster S, or to break the lap record at the Nordschleife, you will be deeply disappointed by the M3W, though, as mentioned, you may give the base-model Caterham a run for its money in a straight line. The M3W's acceleration is brisk, but no more than that.

The test report of the British weekly magazine *Autocar* in June 2012 was highly complimentary in most respects, and the rare overall top rating of five stars was given, but no performance figures were supplied. There was, however, this remark: "Its track acceleration figures show that it's slower than most of its rivals – a 0-60mph time of 8.0 seconds wouldn't have a warm hatch writing home these days ... "

Motor cars are far more intelligent than they used to be, but they still do not write letters. Moving along, the magazine did not mention at the time the reason why there were no acceleration figures. The answer was to be found in an end-of-year review of the "Top 12 cars of 2012":

"So we invited it to our Britain's Best Driver's Car contest, where its suspension broke, quickly, and without warning, on the circuit, of its own accord. Our driver was shaken, but there was no contact. If it had happened on the road, he might not have been so lucky."

The writer of this piece, Road Test Editor Matt Prior, perhaps wishing understandably to erase such an unpleasant incident from his memory, modestly forbore to mention that " ... our driver" had been himself, and that the car had rolled after the breakage. There was a good aspect to this, apart from the driver fortunately escaping injury: Morgan hastened to strengthen the components that had broken. Later, in early 2013, it also stiffened the forward section of the chassis rails, because a number of cars had suffered fractures in that area.

After my M3W was run in and I was able to give it full throttle, I was convinced that *Autocar's* suggestion of 8.0 seconds was almost as pessimistic as Morgan's initial boast of 4.5 seconds had been optimistic.

I wondered about this for a long time. Then, in the July 2014 issue of the American monthly magazine *Car and Driver*, there was a test of the 3 Wheeler, with figures. It was a 2013 model, without the cooling fan or the cosmetic vents in the lower rear part of the bodywork. The magazine recorded 0-60mph in 6.9 seconds, and a standing quarter-mile in 15.5 seconds, at a terminal speed of 88mph/140kph, which is about the same as a base-level Golf GTI. There was also a 0-90mph/145kph time – 17.8 seconds – that illustrates how the little machine's lack of streamlining flattens the acceleration curve above 70mph/113kph.

In the real world, 0-60mph times are pretty meaningless. A car that can do the off-the-line sprint in five seconds will not necessarily be quicker between 20 and 90mph, the measure that matters, than a car that cannot crack six seconds from a standstill, for example.

Nevertheless, 0-60mph figures are good for publicity: it's a benchmark that everyone wants to see, and Morgan is at a

This photograph sums up the allure of the Morgan 3 Wheeler: to drive a wild thing to wild places. The owner of this one, Calum Fraser, an engineer on the oil rigs, is still an M3W fanatic, despite his many problems with the car. (Courtesy Calum Fraser)

disadvantage with the 3 Wheeler. Without having to change up twice, it might be possible to get the M3W's time down to the revised claim of 6.0 seconds, or thereabouts, one-up, and with less than a gallon in the tanks, though it would require a lot of technique and just the right revs, plus a high-grip surface, such as the acceleration straight at Millbrook, to achieve that. Perhaps *Autocar* will have another crack at it one day.

The ratios are more or less satisfactory for the road, but a larger manufacturer with greater resources and bullying power would certainly rearrange them to be able to hit more than 60mph in second gear; a gear-change with a normal manual box will cost at least half a second.

Morgan could, of course, raise the overall gearing by changing the final drive ratio but this would result in a uselessly high fifth gear, and, in the unlikely event that this unaerodynamic little three-wheeled brick could actually hit 120mph, downhill perhaps, there would be a new dilemma: front tyres with a higher speed rating would be required.

I do not think that anyone has yet recorded a maximum speed. *Car and Driver* gave an estimate of 100mph/160kph, suggesting that aerodynamic drag would prevent it going any faster, while the factory suggests 115mph/185kph.

Despite the beast's obvious inability to slice through the air like a hot knife through butter, I should think a true 110mph/177kph would be attainable, and I am not convinced that I would wish to go any faster than that. Even if it were possible to do so, it would be necessary to fit different front tyres, since the Avon crossplies are already very close to the limit of their speed rating of 112mph/180kph (whereas, no matter how steep the hill, unless you fall off a high cliff, the rear tyre is well inside its safety envelope, with a maximum of 130mph/209kph).

So the M3W is certainly not up there with the superbikes or supercars, but, as suggested earlier, it's well into hottish hatch territory, unless you're on an autobahn. It seems improbable that the transmission would be happy to take on an extra dollop of torque, as it already has sufficient problems. On the other hand, some more horsepower toward the top end of the scale would not go amiss. Reprogramming the ECU is certainly possible, but would invalidate the warranty.

A major performance limiting factor is the weight. This little car, if it is a car, though lighter than real cars with four wheels, is heavier than might be expected of something taking up so little road space – it is 126.5in/321cm long, and the maximum width, across the front wheels, is 67.7in/172cm.

I do not know where and how *Car and Driver*, a reputable title of long standing and a big circulation, does its tests. Was the acceleration conducted two-up or with only the driver? Was the fuel tank full or nearly empty? These questions are of little importance in relation to a large, heavy, powerful saloon car. A Rolls-Royce Ghost, for example, hits the scales at 2.4 tons, and it could probably still do 0-60mph in under five seconds with 18 Imperial gallons/82 litres in the tank, four fat plutocrats on board, and the boot stuffed with golf bags.

With the M3W, however, weight is crucial, and the vehicle will be significantly, noticeably, slower when you carry a passenger, and even when the 9.2-gallon/42-litre tank is nearly full because these changes have significantly greater effects on the power/weight ratio. Supposing you weigh about 90kg and your Belgian neighbour weighs 80kg, you will immediately feel the loss of performance when you take him for a blast.

How much does the M3W weigh, exactly, apart from rather more than it should? The MMC's official figure is 525kg, but a Swiss owner put his 2013 M3W on one of his government's official weighbridges and came away with a ticket saying 535kg. *Car and Driver* gave the figure (also for a 2013 model without the Urban Cooling Kit and other modifications) as 1268lb/575kg. Filling the Morgan's tanks adds 30.954kg, so that takes us from 535 to 565. The provenance of the extra 10kg remains an enigma, perhaps a camera bag inadvertently left in the footwell.

Whatever the exact figure, why is the M3W so heavy? The engine, of course, is a heavy lump of aluminium, and once Morgan had opted for an American V-twin there was not much to be done about that. But with its computerised design and engineering facilities, the MMC might have been expected to produce a chassis that was simultaneously less heavy and more rigid. The body/ash frame together do not weigh much. The front hubs and mudguards are seriously chunky, however. But, of course, it is that big shiny twin that is the real culprit.

To get the best out of the M3W, you have to stir the gear lever quite a lot, and keep the revs between 3000 and 5000; the engine does not appreciate labouring under the lower figure, and certainly not below 2700. There's not a lot of point in going above the higher one, except when completing an overtaking manoeuvre. The engine is fairly smooth within this range, as far as a big V-twin can be, with a 'sweet spot' just below 4000rpm. Above 5000rpm, in any case, the torque (which peaks at 103lb ft/140Nm at 3250rpm) is flat-lining, and the power, which tops out at 5250rpm, tails off rapidly after that.

Overheating is to be avoided with an air-cooled engine. Provided you keep moving in the M3W, you will be all right, and in models that have not been fitted with the Urban Cooling Kit (standard from January 2014 onward), it's advisable to switch off the engine if you have to stop at a traffic light or you get stuck in traffic.

The S&S engine does, in fact, have a self-protection system known as 'skip-fire mode.' This kicks in when the engine temperature reaches 385 degrees F (196 degrees C), and switches off automatically when you exceed 5mph or when the temperature has dropped below that level. Skip-fire does what the term suggests, cutting the fuel from each cylinder at regular intervals, so that you get an evenly-timed misfire.

If skip-fire occurs and you are not in an area where you can exceed 25mph/40kph, it's recommended to pull over and allow everything to cool for 30 minutes.

★★★

ECONOMY

Morgan claims 21.1mpg (13.4l/100km) 'Urban' for the M3W, 44.9mpg (6.3l/100km) 'Extra Urban,' and 30.3mpg (9.3l/100km) 'Combined.' The economy figures of car manufacturers generally err towards the wildly optimistic, but this set gives an unusually accurate picture of what you can expect (unlike Morgan's acceleration prediction).

The fuel filler insert lock can be removed if not required. Filling up is a regular nuisance for M3W drivers, as explained in the text.

My driving in the M3W is unlikely to be typical. I rarely get stuck in traffic and tend not to cruise about. I am mostly up in the hills on lightly-trafficked roads. Overall, I have averaged just under 27mpg over a distance of about 2000 miles. During the running-in period, when I was keeping, with deep frustration, between 2700 and 3500rpm as recommended, gradually rising to 4000, I averaged close to 30mpg (9.4l/100km). Since then I have been getting through the recommended 98-Octane (95 is acceptable) at a higher rate, more like 23mpg (12.3l/100km), so very much towards the 'Urban Hooligan' end of the scale, though this has been achieved outside urban areas. I expect that most owners will get between 30 and 40mpg.

Car and Driver recorded 33mpg overall, but that's with big American gallons on board. In Britain, where the more modest Imperial measure is used, that would be 39.6mpg, so they must have done a fair amount of gentle cruising away from the test track. One British owner has stated, to his own surprise, that he achieved 41mpg on a long motorway run. So you can go quite a distance on a full tank if economy driving is your hobby, but the M3W is an odd choice for that.

Filling the 9.2-gallon/42l tank is a recurrent annoyance of M3W ownership. The handsome filler contains a lockable insert, which can be removed and kept in a box in the garage if you do not wish to have it, and aren't morbidly fearful that some feral urchins might maliciously add some sugar. There is no tendency for the system to blow back, which is just as well, as that would cause fuel to flow into the cockpit. So far, so good.

However, not only is the fuel gauge utterly hopeless, showing '0 per cent' when there is about 23 per cent of capacity (2.2 gallons/10 litres) remaining, but the cut-off also occurs prematurely, so it's almost impossible to achieve a consistent level close to 100 per cent. And it

is vitally important not to exceed the prescribed level, because that will make the engine run roughly for a few miles. The fuel gauge nonsense can be improved by fitting a 280mm tank sender. It is surprising that Morgan does not fit it, as it comes from the same supplier. Inaccurate fuel gauges are apparently something of a Morgan speciality. Some traditions should not be preserved.

★★★

TRANSMISSION

Around 115bhp/117ch and 148lbft/200Nm of torque are expelled from the back of the engine. By the time we get to the contact patch of the rear tyre this has diminished to about 80bhp/81ch and 103lb ft/140Nm. Typically, transmission power losses are around 10 per cent, but an examination of the driveline makes it easy to understand why more goes missing in this instance. This is not much at the start of the journey and even less at the end, but as previously mentioned it has caused a lot of problems. From the driving seat, you will not really be aware of all that, provided you follow correct procedure and do not let the revs drop into the lugging zone, below 2700rpm.

First, there's the device that attempts to reduce the violent pulses of the engine. The first 'compensator' was not a big success. The one in my M3W is v2 of that, and although the noises it makes, especially when cold, bother me somewhat, so far it has not let me down, and the failure rate has certainly dropped. I am told that v3, from Centa, has transformed the M3W: those who have bought a 2014 model with it as standard equipment have so far expressed no complaints about reliability, though it apparently still makes clunky noises. These, I understand, are nothing to worry about, as it's as tough as anything north or south of it.

Next along the line is the Mazda five-speeder with its single dry-plate clutch. This is another tough piece of kit that has been widely praised. The gear-change is one of the best things about the M3W, slick and easy, while the clutch allows a smooth take-off. Only reverse gear, set to the right side of the conventional gate, is mildly resistant to selection; well, it is in my M3W, and I do not expect that Mazda gearboxes vary greatly.

The ratios may not be perfect in some respects, as previously mentioned, but that's being a bit picky: it is mainly only as far as clicking the numbers that it can be fairly criticized, though it is worth noting that cruising at 70mph really demands fourth gear to avoid dropping into the lugging zone. A comfortable cruising speed in fifth is around 90mph. Also, in very tight hairpins, first is often too low and second slightly too high, but there is nothing to be done about that; you just have to live with it.

An important point, mentioned without capitals in the M3W service manual is as follows: "A Morgan 3 Wheeler should NEVER tow or be towed." For the first part of that, one may have visions of one of those huge, shiny American Airstream caravans behind a M3W also finished in polished aluminium rolling along Route 66. But you should heed the second part of the message: do not let your M3W be towed for more than a few yards as this will almost certainly destroy something

Early M3Ws, like that with the tan leather, had the gear lever further back than on later versions. The M3W with black leather also has buttons for the optional heated seats.

in the transmission, probably the gearbox and perhaps a few other components, and it will not be covered by the warranty.

★★★★

HANDLING

The evolution of the standard-issue suspension and various modifications which have been provided by the factory and specialist companies is covered in chapter thirteen.

To summarize, though, the original car was fitted with non-adjustable springs and dampers supplied by Suplex. However, demand for the M3W was unexpectedly large, and Suplex's attempts to increase production through a sub-contractor came to nothing, so the MMC switched to Spax. Fitting the Spax springs and dampers, also non-adjustable, necessitated some changes to the front geometry.

The unassisted steering would make parking manoeuvres hard work, even if it were not for the appalling turning circle. Required effort is greatly reduced once you're on the move, though that heavy lump of an engine overhanging the front axle line ensures that it still requires more physical input than some unassisted normal cars weighing a great deal more. It is a very physical machine to drive quickly.

The 3 Wheeler's standard 350-19 Avon front tyres were designed for use on sidecars, so they have soft sidewalls and are not ideal to cope with strong lateral forces. The replacement tyre of choice is from Blockley, with stiffer sidewalls.

Various makes of rear tyre are used. It's a car tyre because it has to be: it gets car-type side loadings, and motorbike tyres are designed for different dynamics. The size is 175/55R16, and most tyres fitted are mildly asymmetric, which seems odd on a single rear wheel, but appears to make little if any appreciable difference; the far wider rear

tyre of the stillborn VW GX3 (see chapter two) was more extremely asymmetric, at least in pre-production form.

Looking at this front/rear rubber combination, you would think that, unless the power can readily overcome the grip of the driven wheel, this thing is going to understeer. And indeed you would be correct: this is the predominant characteristic except in a few particular circumstances. From a standstill or from low speed, you can spin the thing within its own length, but, though there is more front-end grip on dry roads than might reasonably be expected, it is usually the front tyres that will lose adhesion before the wider rear. With Blockleys, there is a tendency to lose grip earlier than with the standard Avons, but the response is more consistent as there is far less sideslip.

You would also suppose that the M3W would not hit the high numbers for roadholding on a test track, and you would again win your bet. *Car and Driver* recorded 0.74g on a 300ft-diameter skidpad, which can generously be described as mediocre. But only someone seriously ill-informed would expect anything better than that. The whole point of the M3W is that it does not 'stick to the road like glue' or 'go round corners on rails.'

I had expected this odd machine to behave as demonstrated by motoring journalist/racer Chris Harris in his Welsh hooning video on the internet. But this proved not to be the case, and it turned out that the later findings of Tiff Needell (racer and motoring journalist) at Cadwell Park on *Fifth Gear* were far closer to my own experience: it is very difficult in most circumstances to unstick the grip of the rear tyre; it just wants to 'push.'

This has nothing to do with the relative abilities of the two drivers: Tiff is just as capable of leery tail-out hooliganism as Chris. However, the cars they drove were significantly different, Harris' car was an of surface will disturb the equilibrium, sometimes indeed more so, especially when both front tyres encounter them simultaneously.

What happens is that as the front suspension compresses or extends, because of the incorrect geometry, the toe attitude of the wheel in question changes, sometimes abruptly. You can observe this very simply with the car static by placing one foot on the front chassis rail and applying pressure: the wheel will toe-in visibly. This should not happen. When this occurs at speed, the driver must hang on hard and fight to maintain position on the road. This can make life difficult in a straight line, but is, of course, more difficult if it occurs mid-corner when the springs, dampers and tyres are already subjected to side forces, and both front wheels are attempting to select a line.

The MMC at first blithely suggested that this behaviour did not constitute a problem, and that it was part of the 'character' of the car. Some owners, who came to be known as 'bump steer deniers,' often shortened to 'BSDs,' on the TalkMorgan forum, agreed with this, occasionally with vigour, even though some of them had never driven a 'five-speeder.' However, under pressure from dissatisfied owners, mainly in Britain and the USA, remedial action began in late 2013, with a simple but effective set of parts called the 'Comfort Pack,' the name inaccurately implying that the problem concerned ride quality rather than roadholding and handling.

Essentially, this modification raises the outer ends of the track control arms, which are then horizontal, whereas in the earlier version the outer ends were visibly an inch lower than at the exits of the rack. An essentially similar but slightly more sophisticated system was introduced as standard at the beginning of the 2014 model year.

Although this fix obviously does not magically cure the incorrect geometry, it certainly brings an improvement, at least in the view of most of us who have had it fitted. Bump steer is more or less eliminated. On the other hand, there is a slight loss of steering feel, especially just around the straight-ahead position, which is why a few owners prefer their vehicles without it. Perhaps they do not attempt vigorous driving on ripply, winding roads.

Having driven home from Toulouse after the long lay-off caused by the failure behind the timing case, I felt that the changes to my vehicle (Comfort Kit, Suplex front springs/dampers and Blockley tyres) had brought an overall improvement. That was on mostly smooth roads. The real test would be on my favourite ride and handling route in the northern part of the Var. I drove on that at the earliest opportunity, and changed my opinion from " ... overall improvement" to " ... transformation."

One particular bend brought the whole thing into sharp focus. It's a fast, third-gear curve, with an inconsistent camber and some surface ripples that are invisible to the naked eye. Before the front-end changes, I had found that, although I could enter this bend with the throttle wide open at a little more than 70mph, I had to fight it all the way as the steering tugged from side-to-side. In case you were wondering, relaxing grip on the wheel and letting the vehicle find its own course was not an option. That would be exit, backwards.

Now, with the modified front end, I entered the bend at the same speed but probably left it slightly faster. That was not the point. I no

This Avon tyre was scientifically shagged by the author in under 2000 miles. Some people have coaxed these sidecar tyres into lasting four times that distance.

early model with the first generation of Suplex dampers, while Needell had the Spax dampers and some geometry changes. The early cars had more neutral handling, and could more easily be steered on the throttle.

Like a number of owners, I was disappointed with this. Except on a damp surface at relatively low speeds, there is not much to be done through technique. You just have to put up with it, or else make some modifications (see chapter thirteen).

Nevertheless, despite the unsound front suspension geometry, the handling is essentially benign and easy to cope with, at least on smooth tarmacadam. As soon as you venture onto less even asphalt, the car's behaviour deteriorates noticeably, however, and this is not confined to potholes or severe mounds. Even small ripples or changes longer felt that I was struggling to stay on the road. After that, I found also that I was more relaxed, or at least less terrified, and I noticed that I was no longer gripping the wheel as tightly.

In my view, the standard Spax dampers work more than adequately overall, but they have a tendency to overheat and lose efficiency when subjected to really hard use. Also, the standard Avons, designed for use on a motorcycle combination outrigger, are not ideal for hard driving. They are highly sensitive to pressure changes, and it is important to keep them inflated to the recommended pressures. There's some detectable roll from the rear end during hard cornering, but it's not severe.

On wet roads, adhesion remains surprisingly good, though there have been reports of aquaplaning in really heavy rain, but most owners will try to avoid driving an M3W in those conditions if at all possible, because it's rather a miserable and potentially frightening experience.

Car and Driver reported that " ... the front tires lose grip without audible complaint." Perhaps the tester drove without a helmet and could not hear much above the noise of the engine. I could hear my Avons even above the noise of the engine, exhaust, and all the rest, while I was wearing helmet and earplugs. Perhaps that blocks out some of the boomy stuff and allows subtler sounds to filter through. The Blockleys are slightly quieter, but still squeal when given the treatment. The wear rate of the Avons indicates that the saying "A squealing tyre is a happy tyre" does not always hold true: I wore mine out in under 2000 miles/3200km. I'm hoping that the Blockleys last a bit longer.

The M3W may be overweight, but you would not think so when you are hit by a strong crosswind at speed. You can be blown off line in these circumstances, and firm steering correction will be required.

My 2013 chassis is more torsionally rigid than the earlier version, but one can still feel some flexing when cornering really hard. Extra bracing has made the 2014 item stiffer, so that has probably been eliminated.

The M3W is surprisingly stable, but you must remember that it has what it says on the package – three wheels – and, in extremis, it will be more difficult to 'catch.' Unlike *Autocar's* tester, whose inversion resulted from a broken wishbone, Eric Hélary, French racing driver turned motoring hack, did not need a component failure to roll. Tiff Needell almost did so when he came back on track after understeering onto the grass at Cadwell Park, and suddenly found more grip than he wished to have. So take care if you decide to indulge in donuts on a wide expanse of car park. These animals can bite back when provoked.

Despite these criticisms, I rate the overall handling as fairly good, even without the 'Comfort Pack,' provided that one does not encounter too many bumps, dips and ripples. But the little machine is far better overall in my view when the Comfort Pack is fitted – and it is still loads of fun.

★★★★

RIDE COMFORT

As detailed under 'Handling,' the bump steer problem is not chiefly a question of comfort, so 'Comfort Pack' is a misnomer. In most respects, the M3W gives a surprisingly compliant ride.

There is the dilemma that when you see a pothole and instinctively get it between the front wheels, as you would with a normal car, you will then traverse it square-on with the back wheel, which sends a jarring thump through the structure.

It's better that the rear should collect it than a front wheel, though, because the latter can result in contact between the track arm and the exhaust header, certainly in pre-2014 models without the Comfort Pack.

Apart from that, the primary ride is satisfactory. Motor engineers divide ride quality into primary and secondary. Primary ride is what the vehicle does over larger bumps or undulations, visible to the human eye and having effects in bump and rebound. With the M3W there is no tendency to wallow over such surface changes, and the suspension settles well after passing over them.

It's the secondary ride, over smaller imperfections with a lower amplitude and higher frequency, that cannot be seen in advance, referred to in the previous section, that cause the problems. This is more to do with steering and handling than ride comfort, though it can at times impart a 'jiggly' sensation to the occupants. In the circumstances, I am almost but not quite inclined to award four stars.

★★★

BRAKES

The only question mark I had concerning the M3W's braking system was why a rear drum is used. One would not necessarily need a rear disc for greater efficiency, but it would make maintenance simpler. However, a disc would complicate the handbrake installation, necessitating a separate cable and calliper, which would also be too costly, and the parts were at hand to do it as it is. The handbrake, incidentally, is of the fly-off type, which is quite useful as a safety device to increase turn-in to a tight bend in extremis.

Outright braking performance is not exceptional, as might be expected from the small overall tyre contact patch. *Car and Driver* recorded 70-0mph in 207ft/53m, which not surprisingly does not place the little Morgan high up the order of merit. For comparison, the figure recorded by the magazine for the 2014 Ford Fiesta 1.0 Ecoboost was 179ft/55 metres. It is always a good idea to plan ahead as far as braking is concerned, but even more so in this case. The M3W can, of course, stop in a shorter distance than a motorcycle. Again, it's a matter of how much rubber is on the road; 70-0mph (without thinking distance) is considered to occupy around 245ft/75 metres on two wheels on a good day.

On a positive note, on a dry surface you have to hit Morgan's pedal very hard to induce lock-up, and even on damp roads the onset of lock-up can easily be detected and dealt with by modulation of pedal pressure or cadence braking in an emergency.

Overall, I'd award almost top marks, though I feel obliged to lop off one star because there is no anti-lock system, which is merely something else to keep the M3W driver alert at all times. The ventilated front discs have never shown any tendency to fade in hard use on Alpine roads in my experience, while pedal weighting is just right, and the feel of what is happening at the contact patches outstanding. The M3W might not always go when you want it to, but it does stop on demand better than might be expected.

Uprating the brakes in some way without going to significantly more grippy front tyres (which might introduce other difficulties) would probably be counter-productive, anyway, as it would almost certainly introduce premature lock-up, and thereby make the vehicle more difficult and less pleasant to drive.

★★★★

ACCOMMODATION

Anyone contemplating a grand tour in a 3 Wheeler is borderline certifiable. It has been done, however, by a few intrepid owners, and with some ingenuity a great deal of kit can be carried in a 3 Wheeler:

its carrying capacity is greater than might be expected from a first glance.

In my M3W, the 'boot,' that container under the beetle back and above the rear wheel, is nearly full even on short trips, with the following items: the standard, minimalist tool-kit bag (containing a large spanner and hammer for the knock-on front wheels); a bag containing other tools (spanners, screwdrivers, Allen keys, Torx drivers, pliers, a Herbertz multi-tool, sufficient wire for half a dozen emergencies, a roll of tank tape, tyre foot-pump, tyre foam can); bag containing warning triangle and 'day-glo' vests; fire extinguisher; plastic five-gallon petrol can; spare front inner tube; spare voltage regulator; camera bag (also containing maps, pullover and scarf); first-aid kit. You may infer from this that I am a pessimist; I see myself rather as a realist and I am

This, more or less, is what you can squeeze ...

... into the luggage compartment of a Morgan 3 wheeler.

The factory's luggage rack is well manufactured. The only objection to it is that fitting it requires drilling through the alleged rollover bars.

sure that M3W owners reading this will agree that it is best to prepare yourself for problems because at some point you will almost certainly have some in your three-wheeling adventures.

An important point that you may soon discover if you get caught out on a rainy day is that this boot looks as if it should be watertight, but it's not. Many owners have solved this by fitting a plastic trailer-mudguard beneath the fibre insert, and this apparently works well. I tend to avoid driving my M3W on wet days, but I got caught out once and my more basic solution – a rag jammed into the rear part of the boot, which seems to be where the water gets forced in, worked well enough.

As well as the boot, there's some useful stowage space on the passenger side under the front cowl, beside the fuse box and the oil tank. Quite a large squashy bag will fit there, or you can install a plastic box. Some owners have fitted locking metal boxes there. On the subject of the cowl, it's held in place by four Dzus fasteners, which are very neat in appearance. William Dzus (born Volodymyr Dzus or Dzhus), an Austro-Hungarian of Ukrainian descent, was a fine engineer, and the installation of his invention in the M3W must have caused him to spin through a least a quarter of a turn in his grave: the forward pair on the front cowl are very fiddly to reattach.

The M3W's passenger, who enjoys generous legroom, can also take a squashy bag of reasonable dimensions under the knees without discomfort. Morgan also offers the option of a pair of side pockets, but these are so tiny they are nearly useless. Several after-market alternatives of better proportions are available. A coin container for motorway tolls is a useful addition, and there is room to Velcro this onto the transmission tunnel ahead of the gear and handbrake levers.

If you need still more luggage space, you'll have to get a luggage rack. With properly designed waterproof bags, an intrepid couple can easily carry enough stuff for two people to go on a fortnight's holiday. I am told that there is little noticeable effect on ride or handling with a 3 Wheeler when fully laden, though it will obviously do nothing for performance and economy. One advantage, apparently, is that it reduces buffeting.

Normally, at this point in a road test, one might examine the efficiency of the heating and ventilation. Of the former, there is nothing to be said; of the latter, it is largely dependent on road speed. Wrap up well on a cold day.

Three stars may seem generous, but what do you expect from such a vehicle? If the first thing that strikes you when you look at a Morgan 3 Wheeler is the shortage of luggage space, then you have undoubtedly missed the point.

★★★

AT THE WHEEL

At first glance, the cockpit design looks very pleasant, and it's undeniable that Matt Humphries and Jon Wells did a good job, considering the limited time and resources available. Over the years, I have been frequently annoyed by road tests in which the writer has asserted that " ... drivers of all shapes and sizes will be able to find a perfect driving position in the Tinbox Climactic," and then I fold my 6ft 3in frame into the alleged exemplar of ergonomics only to find that my head is touching the roof even with the seat set at its lowest, and/or that the steering wheel is too far away when I have the pedals at a perfect distance, and so on.

Similarly, when I test a car, I always try to imagine what it will be like for shorter drivers. Will they be able to reach the pedals, will they be able to see the road ahead, will the top of the steering wheel impede their view?

Only a complete idiot (and alas there are quite a few of those who scratch a living writing road tests) would suggest that ' ... drivers of all shapes and sizes will be able to find a perfect driving position in the Morgan 3 Wheeler.'

In fact, drivers varying in height from quite short to fairly tall can fit into it. I am 192cm/6ft 3in tall, and am near, though not actually at, the limit of the possible. I know of one or two owners an inch or two taller who say that they are reasonably comfortable behind the wheel. A great deal depends on the dimensions of the individual bony parts of your body, specifically thigh-bone length.

Some of these accommodation problems have simple solutions, others not. Let's examine them in detail ...

The M3W is much like a racing car for access and egress, which means that it demands a bit of athleticism and a particular technique. The recommended method, in a left-hand-drive model (transpose left-right for right-hand-drive) is to grasp the further roll-over bar with the right hand, then place the right foot on the floor just ahead of the seat, followed by the left foot.

Next, support yourself by placing your right hand on the transmission tunnel and your left hand on the leather trim on the place where the door would be. Now, keeping your legs straight, slide down beneath the steering wheel.

The steering wheel is detachable, but it is not really necessary to put yourself to the trouble of removing it, unless you suffer from mobility issues (as a result of advanced arthritis, for example). Be warned, though, re-fitting the wheel is a fiddly task. In any case, the

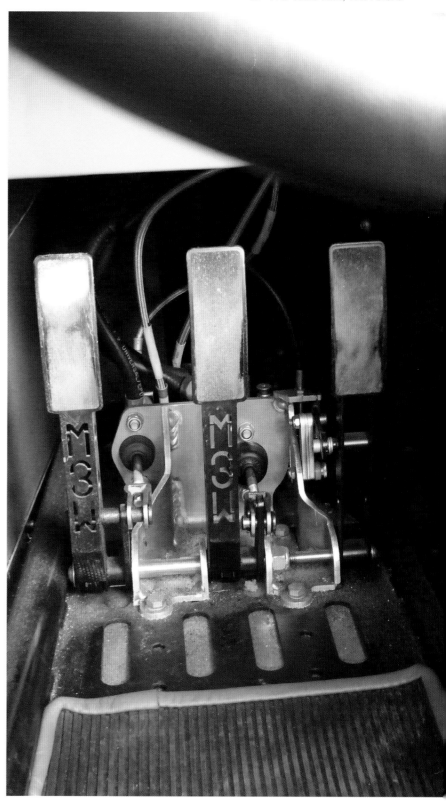

The original pedal assembly gave a nice visual effect but was not ergonomically sound, and was also somewhat frangible.

Back to basics and much better, especially for those with big feet. The revised pedal assembly, introduced in early 2013, is less aesthetically pleasing, but tougher.

wheel is not immediately detachable straight out of the factory. As delivered, one of the three retaining Torx bolts is of the tamper-resistant security type, so you'll need a hollow TT25 driver to remove it (perhaps you'll then decide to replace it with a normal bolt). Once you have fitted a spacer behind the steering wheel, which is strongly recommended, particularly for taller drivers, getting in and out without removing the wheel becomes slightly easier. There's a useful piece of advice in the owner's handbook: "Do not attempt to remove the steering wheel whilst the engine is running or the vehicle is moving."

If you're travelling two up, it's necessary for driver and passenger to get in and out one after another, otherwise you will be in each other's way. Well, you will be slightly in each other's way even so, but it's possible for two large people, possibly even two average Americans, to go places in an M3W, though of course that will have a deleterious effect on the power/weight ratio.

Once in, you must buckle your belt, and this, too, requires some technique. The belt passes across the shoulder at the centre of the car, and buckles beside the outer thigh. You need to take quite a length of belt to be able to lock it, and it's advisable to do this before you put on your gloves.

Now you can switch off your imagination and go places, though there is one further point that needs to be made. The seats are not adjustable, and the only way of accommodating drivers of different heights is by moving the pedal box to one of three positions; let's call them A, B and C. This is not a rapid job that can be effected in a car park in five minutes. Therefore, problems will arise if, for example, a tall position C man is married to a short position A woman, and both wish to drive. Position B will probably not suit either. At position B, I cannot drive the beast; indeed, I can barely get into it, and then it would either be full throttle or hard on the brakes; ie, beyond unsafe.

It's best to choose your driving partner in the way that aristocrats of yore chose their servants: roughly the same height and build as themselves, and taking the same shoe size. This worked out rather well for servants who inherited slightly foxed Savile Row suits and hand-made shoes from Mr Lobb (which they had also worn in with their more robust peasant feet), but there is not yet, as far as I am aware, a website for people to choose sexual partners on the basis of whether the Morgan 3 Wheeler they will share needs to have the pedal box in position A, B or C. Now there's a business opportunity for someone.

To some extent, a compromise can be made by fitting a bolster behind shorter drivers, who may benefit also from having an extra cushion to raise themselves and improve forward visibility. Incidentally, I find driving comfort is improved by raising the forward end of the seat cushion, so that the thighs are better supported.

The M3W's early pedal box was a poor design, and it was replaced early in 2013 with the current, far better version. This is both more robust and ergonomically sounder. The pedals of many modern cars are not well placed for 'heel-and-toe' gear-changing. The term is a misnomer in post-vintage cars, as the heel no longer plays a role in the operation, but it has remained in common use. One side of the right foot presses the brake pedal while the other simultaneously blips the throttle on down-changes for improved smoothness, as this, when performed accurately, ensures that the clutch plates engage at the same rotational speed.

I find that in this respect, the M3W's pedals are perfect, with the throttle angled to the right. However, I take a size 13 shoe and, to my surprise, some drivers with smaller feet have mentioned that the two pedals are too far apart for them. An after-market bolt-on throttle plate or a trip to a racing engineer may be the answer.

The ideal height for the driver of an M3W is probably about 5ft 10in, depending upon trunk length, so that the little Perspex screen is straight ahead at eye level. My line of vision is well above the standard screen, and still slightly above the Fairbourne Carriages screens on my car, though these do reduce buffeting. Even if you are wearing an open-face helmet with the visor down, crosswinds can sometimes not only batter your head, but also make it slightly difficult to breathe, as when walking straight into a strong wind. A full-face helmet probably stops this.

The second problem is that there is nowhere to rest the left foot to the side of the clutch, either in left-hand-drive or right-hand-drive versions. This leads directly to the third problem, in that a tall driver, especially in a left-hand-drive car, will have a problem with the steering wheel: the rim, the left hand, the left knee and the body/chassis all argue over the space. For this there is a simple improvement: a spacer to bring the wheel closer. Several are available. Mine, from Krazy Horse, is 50mm thick and looks like original equipment.

In general, left-hand drive leads to a better driving position, because the right leg then runs straight ahead parallel to the transmission tunnel, while there is usually plenty of space to the left to rest the clutch foot. By chance rather than by design, the right-hand drive version of the 3 Wheeler turns out to be slightly more comfortable for tall drivers than for those with the steering wheel on the other side: with RHD one can more easily bend the left knee when it's not being used to disengage the clutch, because the central console is significantly lower than the body/chassis.

The floor mats look good, but they shift about under the driver's heels. I quote from the handbook: "Footwell carpets should be fastened at all times when driving the vehicle." That is good advice, but here is a fair question: why are they not fastened when they leave the factory? This irritation could be removed by judicious use of adhesive or Velcro, or you can simply remove them and drive around with your heels on bare metal.

The gear lever position on early cars was further forward than on those from 2013 onwards. Opinions of those who have tried both are divided. The lever is in just the right place for my right arm, but this may not be so for those of different dimensions.

A common practice in open cars when the driver is travelling solo is to snap on the half-tonneau over the passenger side. In windy conditions, this can have an unpleasant sail effect, though mostly it keeps the driver more snug. Unfortunately, in the M3W it also makes it even more difficult than usual to read the furthermost dial and the small digital window beneath it, especially for tall drivers.

At a glance, it looks just right ... Note the tiny leather pockets and two non-standard items: Krazy Horse steering wheel spacer and Richbrook gear knob.

So, overall, the M3W's cockpit is quite good, but it's advisable to carefully consider its shortcomings before purchase.

★★★

INSTRUMENTS AND SWITCHES

As with the interior design in general, as mentioned in the previous section, the M3W's instrument display and switchgear look very pleasant at a glance, though once again it's disappointing that there was not a shouty engineer saying, "You can't do that!" from time to time. As with the front suspension, cosmetic allure has been given precedence over practicality.

There are two dials, a rev counter and a speedo, both difficult to read, especially in strong sunlight. Right-hand drivers have difficulty

The odd-looking, leather-wrapped device below the rev counter is the author's patented Max Clifford todger extension for the horn, which otherwise he cannot find in a hurry.

Where function is crushed by form ... (see text).

reading the rev counter through the wheel, and have to look too far to the left to read the speedo. For LHD it's the opposite. Between these dials is the rather silly START button, the bomb release button from the Eurofighter.

RHD customers get a better speedometer, though it is still not terribly good. What one might term the Imperial speedometer at least has markings in logical 10mph increments, starting from 0 and rising to an imaginary 130mph, thus including all the main British speed limits en route. The kph speedometer in metric countries, however, would send Mr Spock's eyebrows into hyperdrive: it also begins at zero, but, as the needle spins around the dial from there, all logic is lost, as there are 15kph gaps between the numbers chosen, as follows: 0-15-30-45-60-75-90-105-120-135-150-165-180 and thence onwards and upwards into fantasy territory: 195 and 210. If this is not utterly daft, I am the Akond of Swat, sailing around on an inland lake.

Of these markings, only 30, 45 and 90 (the second of which would make surely Mr Spock's ears flap, but it is actually a speed limit used by the French authorities, who originate from a different planet) are of any practical use. The crucial markings, corresponding to standard limits, should be 30, 50, 70, 90, 110 and 130 (the maximum allowable on French autoroutes). Why did they not simply copy the dial from LHD four-wheeled Morgans?

The numbers themselves would matter less if the speedo were larger, but its Toy Town dimensions make reading it, even in ideal lighting conditions, somewhat difficult.

There are telltales for the indicators, high beam, engine check and brakes. The owner is advised to read carefully the handbook regarding the possible implications of the latter two.

There's a single stalk on the steering column. It and the line of switches below the dials are handsome devices, aluminium with knurled ends. Apart from its main functions (indicators, headlamp main beam/dip/flash), the stalk has a button on the tip. Unfortunately, this does not operate the horn. Instead, it flips through various digital readouts incorporated within the rev counter and speedo.

These are hard to read at a glance, especially in strong sunlight. As previously mentioned, the gauge gives a percentage readout, but when you get to zero, this does not necessarily mean the tanks are empty. Morgan fitted the wrong sensor, which gives a pessimistic reading, and there will actually be about 3.5 gallons of the full complement of nine remaining in the twin tanks when you first see zero. The other digital indicator, under the rev counter to the right, shows the fuel level. This is even harder to read.

Among all the stuff, some of it of vital importance, that one can blip though with the tip of the column stalk, there is a device for telling the time; yes, one might call it a clock. It is digital and utterly useless. Nobody buys a Morgan 3 Wheeler in order to tell the time, yet it must be admitted that sometimes when driving one needs to know what time it is, and if you're wearing leather gauntlets that reach your elbows, as is advisable on cold winter days, it's not possible to read your wristwatch. Morgan has merely ticked the box on the equipment list without providing a proper solution: it should either be something

that is immediately legible without distraction from the road ahead ... or don't bother at all.

One important thing that can be displayed is a voltmeter, which can provide early warning that the voltage regulator is about to fail, as most of the early ones did. It's something that one needs to know in advance, and there is a good case for it to have a flashing light. There are various flashing warnings, including for the brake fluid level. This is over-sensitive and flashed on my car during hard cornering. The level looked normal, but a small top-up stopped the flashing light.

Below these feeble dials and irritating digitality is a neat line of knurled aluminium switches. From left to right, these are: foglights for those mysterious autumnal forays along the Welsh borders in search, perhaps, of some nice warm muffins; sidelights/headlights; hazard flashers; and horn. Only the last of these is a problem, in my view, and, I think, in that of many owners. With RHD it's obscured by the steering wheel, and with LHD it's too much of a stretch to the right, even if you have simian arms like mine. Various solutions to this literal shortcoming have been adopted. Mine is a special 'todger' consisting of a large plastic dowel, with push-fit assisted by a cocktail stick, covered in the index finger of an old leather glove. I call this the Max Clifford extension; it's only a small thing but it gets the job done. With this, I can instantly announce my imminent arrival on other people's event horizons. Parp! Parp!

It's most unfortunate that Morgan chose not to copy the dash of the Liberty ACE, which was simpler and clearer, as well as being more traditional and, many would argue, as I would, more aesthetically pleasing, as paradoxically often happens when form follows function.

★

NOISE

In the M3W's handbook, under "STARTING PROCEDURE," it's stated that: "When the engine first starts, under certain conditions, the hydraulic tappets may emit a rattling noise." Indeed so, and the Pope may well be a Catholic.

Some owners have complained that the M3W's engine is insufficiently loud. They must be heavy metal fans with perforated eardrums, I suppose. Most people will probably agree with me that wearing earplugs is essential, but even with them inserted, plus a helmet, and, in winter a motorbiking balaclava, you will not be sitting in a quiet place, though it does seem that shorter people, with their ears closer to the ground and out of the airstream, have a slightly quieter ride.

Also, there is apparently quite a variation in noise levels in Morgan 3 Wheelers. There is certainly quite a variety of noise sources. Apart from the grumpy twin-cylinder potato grinder at the front, and the bellowing exhausts from the rear, there are all sorts of whines and booms and rattles, mostly from the various components of the complex transmission.

There is the compensator, to begin with, which has become gradually quieter, as well as smoother in operation, in its three stages of development.

To protect the driveline it is important to avoid combining wide-open throttle and low revs in higher gears, and it's best at all times to keep above 2700rpm. Below this engine speed the whole system becomes rough.

Approaching the advised rev limit of 5800rpm (I have not felt like venturing above that to check if there is a limiter), the sound is of a dozen deranged chefs armed with cast iron skillets having a violent disagreement inside a kitchen lined with steel walls. Some tuned S&S engines emit a beautifully fruity rasp when revved hard, so there is a possibility that one day M3W owners will be able to enjoy a similar kind of mechanical musicality, rather than the thuggish, heavy-metal sound of the present model. But many owners love it just the way it is, so I shall award one more star than my better judgement would allow.

★★★

FINISH

One thing that strikes people when they have only seen the M3W in photographs and then view it close up is how nicely finished it seems to be. Again, a closer look gives a rather different impression in some respects.

A key element of the good part of this is Matt Humphries' design, and the execution of that by Premier. The body panels are very finely made, and although they may have a weight problem, the front mudguards are very attractive, too.

The engine also presents itself well, though it would look far nicer with better quality fuel lines and fixings. Some people object to the throttle cable that rises in a parabola and is visible from the driving seat, but that is rather a traditional feature of Morgans, dating from the early days. It no longer does that on 2014 models fitted with the Urban Cooling Kit.

On the minus side, the front suspension components have a somewhat agricultural and/or locomotive appearance, and those with engineering backgrounds who examine the geometry tend to burst out laughing.

More generally, detail finish is where Morgan lets itself down. Poor-quality screws and nuts and bolts are rather shocking in view of the price. The luggage compartment is not waterproof; neither is the cockpit, even from below. There is work still to be done in these areas.

The instrument layout is also better for display purposes than it is in use. Overall, the interior is quite well finished, however, and the leather nicely trimmed. Incidentally, while Australian versions of the M3W are otherwise uglified, with particularly naff trimmed-down mini-screens, the logic of which is not evident, they do have one rather nice feature: a leather top roll across the fascia, as in the four-wheelers.

★★★

EQUIPMENT: STANDARD AND EXTRAS

Whenever two M3W owners meet up for the first time, they look carefully over each other's vehicle in a game of spot-the-difference. Even ignoring paint colour differences, two absolutely identical 3 Wheelers have probably never left the factory.

This M3W has the Urban Cooling Kit, Blockley tyres, and 'eared spinners' to attach the knock-off (and on) wheels.
(Courtesy Achim König)

As standard, you do not get much more than the bare necessities. The long list of what you do not get would take up many pages. In passing, it's worth mentioning that although there is a rear fog lamp, there is this line in the handbook: "Your Morgan is not supplied with front fog lamps fitted when it leaves the Morgan factory. There is no standard provision to fit them." I take this as wise advice to avoid venturing out on a murky night on the Anglo-Welsh borders (see chapter one). There is no heater either, as previously mentioned. Also as previously mentioned, some things that are provided, such as the clock, one could easily do without.

From January 2014 onward, the M3W has had as standard the Urban Cooling Kit, which clicks on automatically when the huge engine's temperature shifts from very hot indeed to excessively hot, thus avoiding skip-fire mode inconvenience. This does not suck, it blows. It may seem odd that it should blow against the direction of travel, but since it switches itself on automatically only at rest or at very low speeds, this does not matter. Reports on the efficiency of this device (also available for fitting to earlier models) have been entirely favourable, though some people dislike the appearance. Alternatives are available in the after-market.

One useful item that Morgan does provide is a socket, the sort of thing that used to hold a cigarette lighter but which now is mostly needed for recharging mobile telephones or for running satnav systems. It can also be used for plugging in a battery conditioner. One enterprising and/or desperate owner has even used it to rig up a spotlight so that the fuel gauge is more legible after dark!

When buying a Morgan, including the 3 Wheeler, your first stop should be the Morgan Car Company's website: www.morgan-motor. co.uk. Here you'll find a 'Car configurator' which allows you to visualize what your mad dream machine will look like in a dozen basic colours, and also some others that cost extra: in fact, all the colours in the spectrum, even pink or an especially repellent tone of mauve. There is also the option of metallic finishes, and you can splash out on wheels of a different shade than black.

My M3W is about as basic as possible: plain black paint, with tan leather. A lot of people seem to like the extra-cost transfers, especially those with a reference to the RAF, especially the roundels and the bullet holes. The shark look also finds favour. Well, it would be a dull world, etc ...

The thing that puzzles me about the aero part of this is that there is often reference to the Spitfire, which seems to me the wrong aeroplane and the wrong global conflict. If we are with the RAF and World War II, the woody Hurricane would be a better choice. But really, it should be World War I and the ineffably woody Sopwith Camel, an even more scary device than the SE5 of Captain Albert Ball. This would be more appropriate for many other reasons, not least: a) the necessity to suspend imagination before firing up the engine; and b) the feeling of vulnerability even when nobody is shooting at you. When you've done the first of these, that vulnerable feeling never quite goes away; not for me anyway.

After choosing the external look of your M3W, you can select your leather and decide whether you want it pleated or quilted. The standard colour choice is between black or tan but there are a couple of dozen other shades available at extra cost, and you can have the stitching in a contrasting colour.

Next you can see the 3 Wheeler with or without the 'bright pack.' This is by no means given away, but it does usefully increase the visual contrast on the vehicle. It gives shiny coatings to the cowl, headlamp surrounds and alleged roll-over bars. In standard form, the cowl is silver-painted, but you can have it matching the body colour, a good choice in my opinion. You can have the exhaust and/or the heat shield either black or polished. Note that if you choose the polished option for the exhaust, the headers soon discolour because of the hot gases passing through them. Some people dislike this, others regard it as interesting patina. And finally, there are other choices of exhaust design, notably the Brooklands. Well, not quite finally ...

Although you will end up with basic motoring whatever you do as far as the specification of your M3W is concerned, there is nevertheless quite a long list of optional extras; though not including a heater.

So, if you feel you have not already spent enough money, you can add all sorts of stuff. One extra that every owner should specify is a tonneau cover. Standard is black PVC, centrally-zipped, very reasonably priced and of good quality. The more luxurious mohair alternative is not outrageously costly. The heated seats option might also be a good idea, as, oddly, when you have several layers of clothing on your upper half, it's the thigh area rather than the toes that gets cold when the thermometer drops below zero.

From January 2014 onward, the M3W has had as standard the Urban Cooling Kit, which is also available as an after-market fitting through Morgan dealers. Reports suggest that it is highly efficient and not obtrusive in operation. There are alternatives available if the aesthetics of this system displeases you.

Beyond that, there are minuscule leather pockets for the place where doors would be in more ordinary vehicles; you can just squeeze in a mobile phone. There's a bonnet strap which is entirely cosmetic and serves no other function. This is a pity as a proper belt could replace those irritatingly fiddly forward Dzus fasteners. There is an intercom system (but there are far less expensive after-market alternatives), and a Thatcham-approved Toad Immobilizer, which I strongly do not recommend, because it increases the likelihood that the battery will run down as you sleep.

On the advice of my dealer, I did not select the latter option. To his surprise and mine, my M3W arrived with it. Life is full of surprises, some of them pleasant, others not, when you become a Morgan owner. If your 3 Wheeler has the immobilizer, you should follow the advice in the handbook: "Always disconnect the battery or use a conditioner if the vehicle is left for more than 1 week."

You may decide to have taller roll hoops with head restraints. If you are in Australia you will get these whether you want them or not, but the hoops will probably still not be taller than your Barry McKenzie hat with the dangling corks. The Oz hoops are still not braced, so they are still functionally useless.

One thing you may wish to consider while ordering is the option of a 'Photo Build Book,' which means that when you collect your car you will be presented with an album of photos of the various stages of construction, theoretically anyway. Author's advice, based on comments from those who selected this option and ended up somewhere between disappointed and annoyed: if you choose this, remember to nag your dealer and the factory just before and during the build process, lest they forget …

★★

IN SERVICE

If the late Denis Thatcher, MBE, TD, were the author of this book, he might begin this section as follows: "There is a considerable buggeration factor involved in owning a Morgan 3 Wheeler … "

It's probable that everyone who buys a Morgan 3 Wheeler does so in the expectation that they will get a classic type of driving experience, combined with modern reliability. Well, the M3W delivers admirably on the first part of that, especially after a few modifications, but not so well on the second. If you buy one of the trads, you could drive it every day of the year and use it like any normal car, though most owners prefer to save them for special driving adventures.

Apart from all the things that can go wrong, as detailed in chapter twelve, the 3 Wheeler is not especially well adapted to home maintenance, other than engine oil, spark plugs and/or front brake pad changes, though it is easy enough to take off the cylinder heads.

For most other tasks, you need to be a skilled mechanic with a well-equipped workshop. It's possible but awkward to add grease to the compensator (this will not be necessary with the latest Centa unit). Some owners have flushed out and refilled their cars' bevel boxes, apparently with successful results, though if your machine left the factory between November 2012 until 9th September 2013, contact your dealer immediately and check that the bevel box has been replaced. If not, my advice is to do so even if the warranty has expired – and ask for it to be done as if the warranty were still in force. DO NOT put anything in the bevel box other than the recommended lubricant!

It's necessary to let some air out of the tyres to remove the front wheels, because of the curve of the mudguards. The wheels are loosened or tightened by means of controlled violence, using two of the components from the 'tool-kit' – a large spanner and a rubber-headed hammer; the third component is a can of tyre foam, which may help you to get home or to a service station if you drive over a nail, provided you also have a tyre pump.

The front tyres can be changed by any normal tyre-fitting establishment. They have Blockley inner tubes, which can be re-used provided that the reason for replacement is tyre wear rather than a puncture.

As for the rear tyre, as it's of the car type, theoretically it can be replaced by any tyre fitter, but getting the wheel off and on again is a relatively complex, fiddly process, best left to your dealer or to a mechanic with a well-equipped workshop.

The rear tyre tends to hold its pressure, like any normal road-car tyre. Attaching the foot-pump air line is easy enough once you have wheeled the machine so that the valve is somewhere around bottom dead centre. The front tyres, in contrast, have readily accessible valves, but it is advisable to check them before every journey because the pressure does tend to fade slowly.

I have known batteries to expire over the years, but I don't think I've ever previously had a voltage regulator fail. Most of the unfortunate first-year buyers had at least one failure, and although the 2013 model's regulator was improved, it was still not an uncommon cause for roadside misery. My first regulator went after 1600 miles, and the second (apparently part of a bad batch) about 400 miles later. I now carry a spare. Fitting a replacement requires an element of jury-rigging, because at the factory the long wire between the regulator and the 'B+ post' (the insulated earth terminal of the alternator) is comprehensively bound up with other cables.

Checking the oil level of this dry-sump engine is simple: unscrew the cap of the oil tank under the front cowl when the engine is hot – you'll need a glove or a rag to do this – and the oil level should be between the two indicators; early versions had a dipstick, but the later system is far better. My engine used no oil at all for the first 2000 miles, but then it burned off some and required topping up. Apparently, there is a wide variation of usage in S&S engines, and ambient temperature seems to have a strong influence.

One important but very obvious piece of advice: try to avoid doing any work on the engine until it has cooled. The entire front end of this beast becomes exceedingly hot, and it takes a long time to get down to a level at which it is safe to work on.

On the other hand, to check the level in the oil tank, unlike with a wet-sump engine, is to do the procedure when the engine is hot. When the engine is hot, the oil is hot, and you will definitely need gloves to remove the cap. I do not apologise for stating the blindingly obvious in this instance.

I have not performed an oil change, but, apparently, it's quite simple. First, remove the oil feed pipe at the engine, to let the oil tank drain completely. Then remove the sump plug on the bottom of the motor, which also has a magnetic swarf pick-up; only a small amount of oil will run out from here. Then refit and refill.

Many owners have fitted an inner mudguard (adapted from an inexpensive trailer mudguard) between the back wheel and the fibre insert. This apparently keeps the luggage compartment dry, and it also reduces the amount of dirt that can get to sensitive electrical components under that rear cover. It does have the disadvantage of making access to various components – the rear part of the driveline and the rear brake – even more awkward.

Apparently, the 2014 model's reliability is greatly improved in every area, and I have some confidence that the 2015 edition will be better still. However, there should be a paragraph in the handbook advising owners to touch the ash frame for luck every ten miles. I forgot to do that one morning, with unfortunate results.

★

CONCLUSIONS

If you add up all the stars and divide them by the categories, you will

On their grand tour, Mr and Mrs Reid of Dumfries and Galloway in their M3W, with Fairbourne screens, and the Superdry of Monsieur et Madame Mouren of the Var.
(Courtesy Donald Reid/Raphaël Mouren)

Under the front cowl, there is easy access to battery, fuse box, oil tank and brake fluid reservoir. There is also extra stowage space.

see that the average rating is just under three. Yet, despite all the flaws mentioned above, and despite the fact that the first year's owners of the M3W – and many of those from 2013 – quite reasonably consider that they ended up paying for the privilege of being beta testers for the factory, I feel compelled to award four out of five stars overall. If you are wondering, the answer is no, I wasn't paid to do so.

This is probably erring on the side of generosity, but that's because the little beast, when it's running properly, is such a hoot to drive.

Even those who have had some miserable experiences as a result of becoming M3W owners do not deny that. *Autocar* generously gave it five stars, despite the Road Test Editor's unfortunate experience, so this shows that I am not mad, just slightly less generous; or at least, if I am mad, I am not alone. Anyway, I have not started hearing voices yet. Also, I do not have an Advertising Manager hassling me, not that that ever hampered my critical faculties.

★★★★

Chapter twelve

Things that go bump

The various faults and failures that have occurred in the engine, driveline, chassis and suspension of the 21st century M3W have been mentioned here and there in earlier dispatches, but it is probably useful to gather them all together in one chapter. There cannot be the slightest doubt that most of these problems are traceable directly to the rapid, one might say over-hasty, development, and also to an obsession with form that sometimes was given too much emphasis at the expense of function. An extra year between blank sheet of paper and the first completed vehicle rolling off the production line would have made a considerable difference. On a positive note, there's also no doubt that the 2014 M3W is a much more reliable vehicle than the earlier versions.

The owner of a Morgan 3 Wheeler soon becomes accustomed to listening carefully, and warily, to the various noises made by the beast, and hoping not to hear any new ones. It's surprising that anything else can be heard above the raucous roar of the big engine. Yet one does hear these other noises, even when wearing earplugs and a helmet.

When fired up from cold, a lot of high-performance vehicles from before the era of modern electronic control of fuel injection and ignition would start up on several cylinders, the reciprocal and rotational processes proceeding somewhat lumpily before the entire team joined in.

Both cylinders of the electronically-managed S&S engine fire up instantly, if rather clunkily: this is a typical V-twin, so it starts off lumpy and continues lumpy, though it does go through a pleasantly smooth patch either side of 4000rpm once it has been carefully warmed up, which does not take long. The X-Wedge engine has a reputation for being strong and reliable, if not actually bomb proof, provided it is carefully run-in. The 'non-interference' design plays an important role in this, and at least limits the extent of damage when something goes awry inside the timing case.

However, there is one area of weakness: behind the timing case cover – that shiny heptagonal plate with the S&S logo at the front of the engine. Take off this plate and you'll see at bottom centre the crank pulley, and at top centre the intake cam wheel. The camshaft wheels are at the left and right. A robust, Kevlar toothed belt winds its way around all this, assisted by a pair of idler wheels at the top.

It's surprising that the American manufacturer did not thread the front of the crankshaft, so that the nut retaining the timing pulley tightens against it, in the opposite direction of its rotation. This is, after all, an age-old engineering principle. I am also surprised that S&S advises against the use of even a relatively mild (and 'reversible') glue, such as blue Loctite, to keep it all hanging together. I know about this particular mini-disaster from personal experience, as explained in chapter six.

Several cases of timing belt failure have occurred without this forward propulsion of the bolt. One factor in this, it has been suggested, may be excessive build-up of heat inside the casing; some evidence that this is the case was provided in early 2014 when S&S introduced shims behind the casing for ventilation, though I have no idea if this is the real cause of these unscheduled interruptions. It is interesting that Moto Guzzi engines have had a ventilated spacer for some years to reduce the build-up of heat in the alternator.

Heat was unlikely to have been the cause of my engine failure. It was a cold morning, and I had never at that stage driven my M3W in really hot weather, nor had I ever been stuck in stop-start traffic. The engine had never gone into skip-fire mode.

I expect that, as I write this in late 2014, the MMC and S&S know exactly what the causes are, and let us hope that a solution has been found. Moto Guzzi had a similar problem in the first decade of this

A catastrophically cracked early chassis. Happily, this problem seems to have been resolved by various revisions. (Courtesy Calum Fraser)

A bad day on the old RN75, the historic highway between Paris and the south.

The crankshaft sprocket bolt had leapt forward, smashing through the timing case cover.

Inside the timing case: the crankshaft pulley, with its famous bolt, is the one nearest to the road. (Courtesy Nigel Smith)

century, with its new four-valve engine. It seems the first batch had an incorrect washer fitted. There have not been any problems since then.

That's the sole major problem that I know of with this engine, though there have been one or two less serious faults. Hoses have come loose and sprayed fuel back towards the cockpit, some sparkplug leads have become semi-detached, and some electronic control units have needed replacement. Higher-quality fuel hoses and connectors would be a welcome upgrade.

The voltage regulator caused numerous early breakdowns. Its improved specification and mounting (to eliminate vibration) have reduced the likelihood of this. The regulator/rectifier sometimes fails when the ground wire severs through vibration; the unit was mounted to the engine cradle, which subjected it to vibrations for which it was not designed, rather like wearing a self-winding wristwatch while operating a pneumatic drill … and sometimes it just fails.

The 'fix' is a supplementary ground cable to back up the original. This works well enough, but remounting would be preferable. Also, the vibration isolating bobbins are notably poor, and crack regularly … there are better types available. The 2014 M3W's rectifier is better insulated from vibration.

Exhaust pipes have sheared, through a combination of vibration (those massive torque spikes wreaking havoc here, there and everywhere) and poor-quality mounting bobbins (the same low-grade type used for the voltage regulator). These bobbins were probably designed for fitting between the chassis and body of Edwardian perambulators, and for such a task they would almost certainly prove adequate. Again, these have been improved since the early production cars, and that seems to be another problem solved. There was a particular concern about the distinctive Brooklands exhausts which have been especially snappy, but the strengthened 'Mark 2' design seems to have put a stop to that.

On all M3Ws, between the exhaust headers and the catalytic converters, there is a short section of flexible woven steel fibre. The intention of this was to absorb a lot of the twisting motion of the S&S. It is indeed very flexible, and it was an intelligent idea to fit it, but on its own it was insufficient. All seems to be well so far in that area.

Downstream from the engine, greater difficulties have arisen, either side of the Mazda gearbox, which seems so far to have been a model of reliability despite the undeniably harsh environment in which it has been installed, with things ceasing to function either side of it.

The early compensator, as previously noted, was a poor design, cobbled together in a hurry and subject to numerous failures. The second generation was significantly better, but still far from perfect. If your compensator starts to make excessive noise, consult your dealer at the earliest opportunity. It may need an extra injection of grease. The earliest version was puzzlingly nipple-free, however. The Centa unit fitted from 2014 onwards seems to have resolved all these problems.

Provided that a modification can be found to stop that crankshaft pulley bolt becoming loose, all but the most unlucky should have a 3 Wheeler that is satisfactorily reliable from the front to as far back as the exit of the Mazda gearbox. Reducing the probability factor of roadside despondency caused by these driveline failures, large and small, would be a major step forward.

Quaife is a company with a very good reputation and considerable experience of making all sorts of gearing systems. Therefore, even though the M3W's bevel box was custom-built, I was very surprised that it was the cause of so many problems, ranging from the minor but irritating, such as excessive noise, to the potentially disastrous: a few bevel boxes have failed, some of them actually seizing during use. There is a simple explanation of this phenomenon. I do not know the date of this directive that was sent to all Morgan dealers:

"During the period between November 2012 until 9th September 2013 an additive was combined to the bevel box oil on all M3Ws. This additive over a period of time has been found to bond with the oil and forms clumps within the box, this can result in the gears not getting sufficient lubricant when required. It is essential that vehicles produced between these two dates have the bevel box oil changed, we recommend turning the rear wheel while filling with oil to flush any debris through the system (obviously as we recommend this is done at first service 1000 miles or three months, whichever is first, all affected vehicles should now have passed through there [sic] dealer and the oil changed)."

Quaife Engineering denied knowledge of this when I asked about it shortly after this was posted on the TalkMorgan M3W forum in July 2014. Happily, no one was injured as a result, and it's highly unlikely to happen again. As one dealer told me, "The box is built to the hilt by Quaife, and there is no other reason for it to fail now. The thing should accept several times the horsepower beyond what it's dealing with."

If you suspect that your bevel box is among the 500 or so affected by this (I was understandably relieved that mine narrowly missed this potential hazard), you should have it stripped, checked and probably rebuilt or replaced, rather than merely flushed and refilled. This is perhaps the most vital component in the M3W because, in the event of seizure, there's nothing you can do but sit there, try to steer, and hope for the best; de-clutching will do nothing and braking may even make the situation worse.

At the exit of the bevel box is a small sprocket. As this turns, it drives a belt that turns the larger sprocket attached to the rear wheel. The belt is literally made of tough stuff – carbon fibre – and it is, in fact, so tough that it looks for a weak link, which turns out to be the rear sprocket. Apparently, this will soon be made of a harder material, anodized steel rather than aluminium, so that should stop that problem.

There have been a few rear wheel bearing failures, the approach of which is signalled by steadily increasing noise. The cause of this is that the standard bearing is of a motorcycle type, not designed to withstand the lateral force that is normal for a car wheel. Once this bearing has been replaced with a more sturdy item, there should be no repetition. This is another change that the MMC should introduce to its production line.

Chassis/suspension failures affected only the early M3Ws with the thinner-gauge chassis tubes. It's not known how many failures of this kind occurred, but not enough to make it of concern to the DVSA (Driver and Vehicle Standards Agency), which carefully monitors such things. There have been no accidents and no one has been hurt.

Some 2012 M3Ws covered as many as 10,000 miles before cracking. The majority of these problems seem to have occurred in the British Isles, and it has been suggested that the poor state of the roads has been a significant factor. Driving style may be another. It's hard to tell, but happily it's no longer something to worry about, except for owners of unmodified early examples.

I had imagined that the worst thing for the chassis would be a combination of awkward road shocks, but apparently this is not necessarily so. Mark Edge of ABT, the chassis manufacturer, explains: "I am led to believe that the worst thing you can do is just to leave the engine idling, that is when it just running on its own power. That is when the most vibration is generated from the two pistons firing and time between is longer. At the higher revs when driving the vibrations are lessened."

Those who no not have the Urban Cooling Kit or a similar device may be tempted to switch off the engine when they are at traffic lights or otherwise obliged to come to a halt. However, this is probably a bad idea, because it could drain the rather low-spec battery if you did this too many times in a row. In any case, the strengthening of the chassis – even the interim improvement from late 2012 onwards – appears to have cured the tendency of the tubes to fracture. Also, the engine is at its most vibratory immediately after you press that bomb release button.

Supposing you buy a 2012 M3W, it is possible to have factory upgrades or replacements of various components, such as a new reinforced chassis, the 'Comfort Kit,' and driveline components. This should be discussed in detail with the dealer.

What else can go wrong? Well, all sorts of things: failing voltage regulator, dead battery, melting front indicators, and so on and so forth. But let's not become paranoid. Get it sorted, get it back on the road and have fun.

I am confident that the MMC has resolved the M3W's teething problems. Let's hope so, for its own benefit, and that of future buyers of this remarkable piece of automotive weirdness.

Chapter thirteen

Dynamic improvements

As has been previously mentioned, Morgan's development team did not like the aesthetics of the Liberty Ace's front suspension, particularly the positioning of the steering rack in front of the engine. "We thought that made it look too much like a kit car," said Mark Reeves.

There was never any consideration of using sliding pillars, as on all Morgans to date except for the Aero series and its recent derivative, the new Plus 8. That would have added more weight, and besides, Morgan wanted the new car to look 'retro' but to behave more like a modern car. The switch from Harley-Davidson to S&S also caused installation complications, because of its wider vee, as well as the other difficulties that have previously been discussed.

In its development phase, the M3W was fitted with non-adjustable Suplex coil-over dampers. Early production cars were so equipped, but Suplex, which had been given an initial contract for only 50 sets, lacked the capacity to meet the unexpected demand that occurred following the launch; which caught everyone concerned by surprise.

Suplex attempted to increase supply to Morgan via a subcontractor, but this failed to materialize. The MMC turned instead to Spax, whose springs and dampers, also non-adjustable, have been the standard fitment ever since. Through no fault of Spax, installing this altered suspension required the ride height to be raised, and required some geometry changes which made an already unsound configuration worse and exacerbated the bump steer problems.

Instead of designing the suspension and steering specifically in search of the best possible dynamic behaviour, Morgan admits that the design of these components was led more by 'cosmetics' than by engineering. Thus, the 3 Wheeler has equal-length, asymmetric upper and lower wishbones, with the forward links at 90 degrees to the direction of travel.

You didn't need a degree in engineering to detect the fault. All you needed to do was to stand on the chassis rail: as the suspension compressed, the front wheel toed inward.

The most serious flaw of this arrangement was that the track rods in standard pre-2014 models were not horizontal, the outer tie rod ends being visibly and significantly lower than the rack. Early cars could be made to oversteer with heavy application of throttle, as shown in a video made by motoring journalist/racing driver Chris Harris. However, racing driver/television presenter Tiff Needell, driving a later car at Cadwell Park for the *Fifth Gear* programme, tried hard and failed to overcome the inherent understeer.

Lee Cliff writes:

"When I took delivery of my car in February 2013 I was far from impressed with the steering in all respects: I felt it was trying to kill me at any and every opportunity. This is not an exaggeration. The slightest undulation or sunken manhole cover would have me heading for the kerb or over the white line. This to me was wholly unacceptable, but no one seemed to be doing anything about it.

"I measured the front geometry to see what was going on. I have a reasonable idea how to set a car up, as I had competed in a number of speed championships in the past and have always done my own preparation and setup.

"As it came from the factory, static unladen toe was three degrees positive, ride height was 135mm. Bump steer was 0.675in with 1in of bump and ´1in of droop. Anything more than 0.030-0.040 would need rectification. In effect, the front wheels were turning at random, and independently of each other.

"Further investigation highlighted that there were two remedies for this situation: either lower the car by 35mm (this levels up the steering arms) or raise the steering arms by the same amount. I designed such a device and made up a dummy to carry out a static test. This reduced bump steer to about 0.030in. I was about to have some adaptors machined, but the car was booked in at the factory for the first service so I took my drawing and test data with me.

"I spoke to several people at MMC on the day and gave them the drawing, told them to make a pair of adaptors and try it on a car, because I knew it would cure the fault. I thought, if all M3Ws were handling like mine did, it would only be a matter of time before someone was injured or killed. Also I supposed if they did I might get a pair for free!

"Much to my surprise, the Comfort Kit appeared not long after,

with a few slight modifications to aid mass production, and not even a thank-you for me, let alone a free kit.

"I have gone down route 1, I have fitted the Spax adjustable dampers and lowered the car to 100mm front and 110mm at the rear, toe is set at zero degrees. It now steers like it should have all along."

As covered elsewhere, even without the bump steer issue, the dynamic behaviour of the front end of the M3W featured high on the list of its development problems. Early wishbones and uprights were fragile, and the chassis also flexed too much (and in some cases it fractured under the stress).

It has been suggested that the early Suplex cars did not suffer

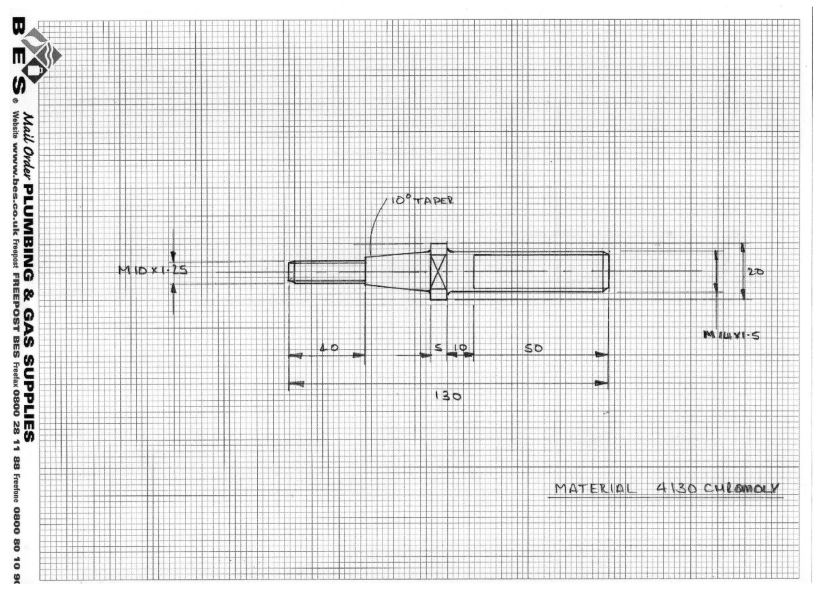

Lee Cliff's drawing of his proposal for a simple device to cure the bump steer of the early M3W. (Courtesy Lee Cliff)

Morgan's Comfort Kit, here fitted to the M3W of Donald Reid, closely resembles Lee Cliff's drawing. Note also the wrapped exhaust headers.

from bump steer, though Pete Larsen disagrees: "Our 2013 demo came fitted with non-adjustable Suplex, and, coupled with the bump steer and kick-back, the car was nearly uncontrollable on medium rough roads. I was given the answer from Morgan 'Oh, we had a bad batch,' but when replaced with the now standard Spax, the car was transformed."

However, raising the ride height and geometry changes made for the installation of the Spax dampers introduced some problems on

The optional Suplex front springs/dampers, adjustable for stiffness.

uneven surfaces. When the suspension is compressed over a bump, the front wheel concerned toes in significantly; when it extends, the wheel toes out. These effects give the driver a lot of work to maintain control in certain circumstances.

M3W owners have complained that they have acted as beta testers for the factory, but some owners have actually gone further than that and become voluntary development engineers. The so-called 'Comfort Kit,' for example, is closely based on a design by Lee Cliff, an English heating engineer, who bought his 3 Wheeler in 2012.

The bump steer issue caused some controversy, and it took a while for the MMC to agree that action was required. Gradually, the 'bump steer deniers' became less vociferous.

As previously mentioned, my view of the Comfort Kit is almost entirely favourable. When it was fitted I also had the front toe set to zero, whereas previously it had two degrees of toe-out on each side, as had been the factory's recommendation. This toe-out was, I am sure, the reason for the asymmetric wear pattern on my front Avons – they were noticeably more shaven on the inner edges.

The 2014 model, as well as having an advanced form of the Comfort Kit, has redesigned uprights, which, I am assured, bring

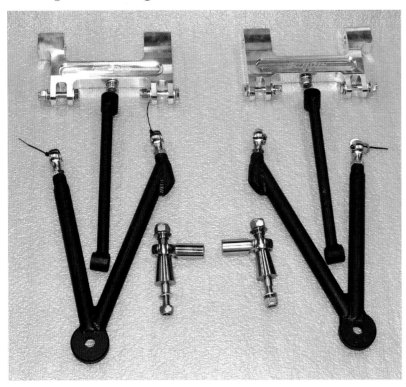

The Empire Kit, manufactured by hillclimb specialist Bill Chaplin, ready for installation. (Courtesy Paul Jacobs)

a further improvement. My view, as previously expressed, is that replacing the original Avon tyres with Blockleys is very worthwhile.

After that, the next components for consideration are the springs and dampers. If you're a medium-pace driver, the standard Spax setup will probably be satisfactory. The harder you drive, the more you'll experience understeer and the more likely you are to overheat those dampers.

At the time of writing, there are only two upgrades that I know of: Spax or Suplex. Both have modified springs combined with adjustable dampers. The Suplex setup is more sophisticated, but also considerably more expensive. I have not tried the modified Spax system but reports have been favourable.

My choice was Suplex, and I am very pleased with the results of its front-end kit. However, I am not the only one to have had problems with the rear Suplex springs, which, when I tried them with the dampers set relatively soft, gave an unacceptably harsh ride. As I write, Suplex, which is a long-established and experienced company, accepts that there is a problem, which it is investigating. By the time you read this, whatever caused the problem will have been resolved. Speak to your dealer or directly to Suplex.

If you go for the front-end kit, the rear set, properly sorted, would be advisable, because that should allow adjustment of the handling balance to reduce the inherent understeer.

Apart from being adjustable (theoretically!) Suplex's 2014 optional units differ from the original set as follows, according to Dan White:

"The concept of controlling roll at the front and pitch at the rear with internal rebound springing is identical. Spring rates were very slightly revised: up five per cent at the front, and the rears introducing a progression in order to accommodate additional load. Rate at static is unaltered. The damper characteristic [of the newer set] is a little more sophisticated."

Pete Larsen told me, "In my opinion, no proper solution may be reached without new uprights which feature greater king-pin angle and corrected wishbone lengths." I am sure that this is essentially correct. Nevertheless, the modifications described above make a considerable overall improvement.

A modification definitely worth considering is the Empire Kit. This was originally commissioned by M3W owner Paul Jacobs, who knew Bill Chaplin of hillclimb specialist Empire Racing through his competition experience. Paul explains: "The Empire Kit corrects the length of upper A-arm to the length of the tie rod, and puts them in basically the same arc during suspension travel.

"This is the missing key in the Comfort Kit ... unless you correct the upper A-arm length, they (tie rod and upper A-arm) aren't swinging in the same arc ... granted the Comfort Kit hedges it closer to being right by elevating the end of the tie rod, but it is nowhere near arriving at really being right."

The Comfort Kit addressed only the height of the steering arms, to bring the track rod up to an acceptable level. This vastly reduced the amount of kickback going through to the steering wheel, but has not completely removed the change in camber or toe. With the Comfort Kit fitted, the front wheel barely moves when you put your weight on the front of the chassis.

With the Empire Kit, there is no movement at all. As Paul explains: "What the Empire Kit does is to go one step further, and completely correct the whole front end geometry, so that like practically every car on the road, unequal length wishbones are employed, which means that with the revised pivot points, the top and bottom wishbones as well as the steering track rod all describe exactly the same arc of movement, and so the wheel stays exactly upright or in the position it has been set at, which is normally around 1.5 degrees of negative camber, and the toe also stays the same, no matter what the suspension is doing.

"The fact that it is fully adjustable by the very simple use of two spherical joints is purely an added facility for those who want to play around with their adjustments. I have not touched mine since I got it from Empire, but I am hearing of very interesting results by going to more camber, which appears to give more front end grip – that we desperately need to reduce the understeer inherent with the basic design."

There is or has been a problem with combining the Empire Kit and the optional Suplex adjustable dampers/coil springs. If you're planning to fit both of these modifications, you should consult both Empire and Suplex before taking your tools out of the box.

A note of caution: at the time of writing, the Empire Kit is not officially recognized by the MMC. This does not mean that it disapproves of it, but it does mean that you should tread carefully

The Empire Kit installed, in optional black version. Note the quality of manufacture. The kit corrects the front suspension geometry and is fully adjustable. (Courtesy Chas Saunter)

concerning the legal implications, particularly concerning insurance. It was this that made me decide against fitting it. I have urged the management of the MMC to examine the Empire Kit with a view to offering it as optional equipment. Ask your dealer whether the situation has changed.

VISIT VELOCE ON THE WEB – WWW.VELOCE.CO.UK
All current books • New book news • Special offers • Gift vouchers • Forum

109

Chapter fourteen

Making it better

First essential with an M3W is to make yourself comfortable behind the wheel, or as comfortable as is possible. The problem of drivers of varying heights sharing the M3W, mentioned in chapter eleven, should be considered carefully before purchase. Fitting a backrest cushion seems to work well as a compromise for shorter drivers, though the MMC advises against this.

One fault that cannot be resolved concerns the pedals. They are of an excellent design, just like in a good competition car, and provided you wear proper shoes you will not have a problem, even with oversized feet (I take size 13 UK/14 USA/49 EU). However, there is nowhere to rest the clutch foot, whether the car is LHD or RHD.

You have to bend your left leg more than is ideal when you're not actually operating the clutch. As mentioned previously, I found immediately that this brought my knee and my left hand (it would be the right knee and hand for those in RHD models) into conflict with wheel and bodywork. I was relieved to find that several people manufacture and/or supply spacers, in various sizes. Mine is 50mm and I bought it from Krazy Horse, the motorbike and Morgan specialist of Bury St Edmonds, Suffolk. It looks like original equipment and makes an enormous difference.

Fitting the spacer took five minutes, but you must first remove the factory-supplied security bolt from the steering wheel, which you will need to do anyway if you wish to remove the wheel for access. It's worth raising the front of the cushion by several inches, for improved thigh support.

Volodymyr 'William' Dzus (1895-1964) was a brilliant engineer. It is not his fault that the fasteners that bear his name have caused irritation to M3W owners: getting the front cowl off is no problem, and it looks very neat when closed; refitting is more difficult.

A steering wheel spacer is not a panacea for the driving position problems, but it does improve matters for tall drivers.

Ingenious solutions have been proposed, including the use of either clips of some kind (small clothes pegs, for example) or split pieces of plastic tubing. In each case, the idea is to hold out Mr Dzus' clever fasteners so that they do not get stuck. This has apparently

The Brooklands steering wheel is a popular extra-cost option. It can also be covered in leather, but that is even less inexpensive. (Courtesy Blake Marvin/MMC)

There are more attractive after-market alternatives to the standard S&S air filter, as shown here on Chas Saunter's car, which also has full brightwork. (Courtesy Chas Saunter)

O

The standard Mazda gear knob looks out of place in the M3W. Also, the gap between the gear lever and the fly-off handbrake lever is marginal.

worked quite satisfactorily for some people, but it still seemed annoyingly fiddly to me.

I had seen on TalkMorgan a car fitted with rather fine-looking chromed cowl clips (also used on the Liberty ACE). I approached the UK Morgan dealer who had supplied them. He quoted for a set of four (adding that he was out of stock). I replied that I would get back to him if I grew an extra limb.

Internet surfing provided identical clips at one quarter of the price. I wanted only two. I was nervous about drilling into Premier's aluminium panels, but the job is easier than anticipated. I felt reasonably confident because the basic procedure is the same as for drilling through glazed tiles, which I had learned from a DIY book. I kept the rearward Dzus fasteners, because they work correctly. Like most gods, Dzus is sometimes let down by his followers.

Many people dislike the standard steering wheel. The size seems just right to me, and although some wood-rimmed alternatives look very nice, I prefer the leather covering for secure grip when seriously cornering; that is less vital with the Comfort Kit fitted.

In one of my early drives in the M3W, the gear lever knob (a Mazda item) flew off. The grub screws had loosened. This inspired me to replace it with a better-looking Richbrook knob.

In France, it is obligatory to display an insurance slip (road tax is no longer levied, but may return). I copied what the bikers do (see photo).

Numerous other improvements have been made by ingenious owners. These can be viewed on the TalkMorgan forums.

The biker solution to displaying an insurance slip (as here) or tax disc. Note also in this photo the pre-Comfort Kit position of the end of the steering arm.

Chapter fifteen

The sales story

The Morgan Motor Company produced 977 vehicles in 2013. That's almost 19 per week; a figure that would have pleased Sir John Harvey-Jones. The 3 Wheeler, in its first full year of production, accounted for almost 45 per cent of the total.

Of these 438 M3Ws, 356 of which were the standard model, with special editions making up the remainder, 40 were the Superdry (a collaboration with a trendy clothes manufacturer), and 21 each were Gulf and Brooklands editions.

The 1000th 'five-speeder' left the factory in January 2014. The production rate of 3 Wheelers for the first eight months of 2014 averaged around 6.5 per week, so one can anticipate that the total for the year will be somewhere around 325.

This reduction (against the trend of increased production in the UK motor industry during that period) can probably be attributed to the reliability problems of early cars. Now that the occurrence of faults and failures has been greatly reduced, demand should begin to pick up again, unless the M3W was just a fashion spike and is now subsiding. I doubt it.

The M3W has so far been sold to dealers in 25 countries: the UK, USA, Dubai, New Zealand, Hong Kong, Japan, Australia, China, South Africa, Philippines, Switzerland, Holland, Italy, Sweden, Denmark, Germany, Belgium, Luxembourg, France, Latvia, Norway, Portugal, Austria, Spain, and Czech Republic. Australia is about to join the club, and no doubt others are on the way.

In August 2014, Steve Morris said: "We are just about to get into Australia, and that's going to be very big for us. There have been 500 expressions of interest there." The Morgan dealer in Australia, Chris van Wyk, based in Melbourne, has a reputation for achieving a high conversion rate.

Morris says that, "The biggest problem facing us as a company is the different legislation in the various countries in which we operate. The hardest thing for us in Australia was the noise test. Noise tests are rather unrealistic, but you have to pass them – so you have entry speeds, exit speeds, with every variation of exhaust that we produce."

The Brooklands Edition. The exhaust system of this has had an unfortunate tendency to fracture, despite strengthening measures.

A Gulf Edition, with black-coated exhaust.

Chapter sixteen

The M3W in competition

In the 1920s, Morgan 3 Wheelers were formidable competitors in motor sport. A skilled driver in an Aero was often able to beat far more powerful opposition. Their advantage was simply their lightness, which gave them an excellent power/weight ratio.

Times and, especially, tyres have changed. The 'five-speeder' does not have a particularly good power/weight ratio. Despite its extra wheel, the Seven 160, least powerful member of Caterham's range, weighs a lot less (490kg/1180lb claimed), which cancels the Morgan's power advantage (it develops about 15 per cent more bhp at the flywheel). The straight-line performance of the two vehicles is quite similar, though the baby Caterham does the brick-wall act at 100mph, which would let the Mog get by on long straights.

Put them on a circuit, other than Le Mans or an oval, and the Morgan has no chance. It's the front tyres that make the difference: it would be interesting to see how well the Seven 160, perhaps the modern equivalent of an Austin 7 Ulster, would cope if it had to run on 3.5in wide front tyres, even with some suspension tweaks.

By an odd coincidence, my brother recently restored a 1932 Austin 7, and it has 19in wheels, which he has fitted with exactly the same Blockleys as on my Morgan, though they do not have to work so hard on the Austin, even with him at the wheel.

Looking at this comparison in another way, it would require more than some minor suspension tweaks to make the M3W work properly if fitted with front tyres as wide as the Seven 160's, which do not give a Bigfoot footprint by modern standards. Despite this, the five-speeder is gradually becoming a more common sight in sprints and hillclimbs.

Andrew English gave the 21st century 3 Wheeler its competition debut at the Cholmondeley (pronounced 'Chumley') Festival of Speed on the 16th of June 2013. Rather oddly, because the organizers obviously wanted the Morgan presence but were puzzled about where to place it, he ran in the sidecar class. Perhaps they looked at those Avon front tyres. In this standard 2013 model, English finished fourth in a field of eight, but here is proof indeed that comparisons are odious. The field included a four-wheeled GG Quadster, which set the best time, and a GG Taurus (the same thing but with only one rear wheel) was second fastest.

Meanwhile, Mark Reeves was preparing one of the early 3 Wheeler test hacks for competition use. His first outing was the hillclimb at Loton Park on the 21st of April, 2014. With Joanna Wallace crouching out of view in the passenger seat, he set the best time in his class, which consisted of seven Morgans that left the factory between 1927 and 1950.

However, several in the 'racing class' were a lot faster. The top drivers in this are Hamish Bibby and Bill Tuer, who often drive the same crazily quick 1932 Aero. It should be mentioned that this runs on 'funny fuel,' not at all like the ordinary pump stuff in Reeves' car. Bibby's best-time-of-the-day was almost 4.7 seconds faster than Reeves' time; a big gap over a course only 1475 yards (1349 metres) long.

Gradually, Reeves has modified the beast, and is getting closer to the times set by the lightweight ancient machines. At the La Vie en Bleu (blue for Bugatti) meeting at Prescott on the 25th of May 2014, with Managing Director Steve Morris spectating, Reeves was within two seconds of Hamish Bibby's best time.

Some of Mark Reeves' experiments may eventually filter down to the production line, but not his first weight-saving measure: he removed the heavy front mudguards. After putting the front Avons to the extreme slip-angle test (in photographs they looked to be on the point of peeling off the rims), he then switched to 18in-diameter wheels with slightly wider tyres.

The biggest change he has made so far has been to fit the more powerful 128in³ engine, which is now an option (rather expensive) for M3W buyers. The best thing about this is that this combination of extra power, increased grip from the front tyres, and Reeves' aggressive driving style should be useful for development purposes. If he can't break it, it probably won't break.

At the time of writing, the regulations for the 'five-speeder' in competition are about to be adjusted, so check with the MTWC or the TalkMorgan 3 Wheeler forum for the latest information.

The modern M3W will never achieve the sporting successes of the Morgans between World Wars I and II, but it's splendid that owners have the chance to enjoy themselves and entertain spectators in hillclimbs and sprints.

Left: Andrew English leaps a factory-supplied Gulf Edition over the
humpback in the M3W's competition debut at Cholmondeley in 2013.
(Courtesy Richard Gilbert)

Above: A year later, also at Cholmondeley, Andrew English on the startline
    in Mark Reeves' potent modified M3W. (Courtesy Jay Stride/MMC)

Loton Park, Shropshire is 1475 yards long, and one of the most demanding British
    hillclimbs, with an average gradient of 1 in 25; the steepest section is 1 in 7.
                        (Courtesy Loton Park)

Joanna Wallace, Mark Reeves' brave passenger. Unlike vintage three-wheeler passengers, she does not have the job of maintaining fuel pressure to take her mind off tyre squeal, flailing arms, and the unfolding horizon. (Courtesy Jay Stride/MMC)

A slice of Morgan history in one frame: Mark Reeves' highly modified modern machine sandwiched between an F4 and a Super Sports. (Courtesy Jay Stride/the MMC)

Reeves' highly modified 2012 M3W, with 128in³ engine, reduced ride height, adjustable dampers, smaller wheels, and no mudguards. Note the slip angle of the loaded tyre. (Courtesy Jay Stride/MMC)

Main pic: At the startline at Prescott. Reeves' machine has the optional raised rollover bars fitted with leather pads. (Courtesy MMC)

Inset: For Prescott, Reeves had found more suitable tyres. The right front tyre is heavily loaded (note compressed spring) but is not threatening to peel off the rim.

Prescott Speed Hillclimb course in Gloucestershire rises 200ft over a distance of 1127 yards.

Chapter seventeen

What to wear when three-wheeling

There are two crucial areas of the body in relation to this chapter heading – stop that sniggering at the back – I mean, of course, the head and the feet.

Taking it from the top, there are some who drive M3Ws without a helmet, which is unwise, or even without goggles, which is simply daft. Even if you are quite short, the standard little perspex screens cannot be guaranteed to protect your eyes against insects and dust, not to mention birds and flying stones. In any case, in many countries a helmet is a legal requirement for those driving the 3 Wheeler, because it's classed as a motorcycle.

I prefer an open-face helmet, and mine has a double visor, the main one clear and the secondary one behind it darkly tinted. However, I soon found that the tinted visor was insufficient, even when I wore sunglasses, at times that the fierce Sun en Provence was low in the sky.

I found a simple solution, borrowed from racing drivers of years past (I'm not sure if they still do this): I attached a 2in/5cm strip of tank tape across the full width of the top of the clear visor. Then, all I need to do is to dip my head when heading into the sun. Believe me, this works; as would a peaked helmet.

Some people also drive without earplugs, which I think is odd. Perhaps my hearing is hypersensitive, or perhaps they are already a bit deaf, though I think my height makes a significant difference to received noise: my ears are up in the airstream, whereas a shorter driver, sitting lower, is perhaps more insulated from the sound waves emitted by the uncouth blare of the exhaust.

In winter, I wear a motorcyclist's balaclava, and often a neck warmer, since, again, my height exposes me more to the rush of cold air.

Moving to the opposite extremity, it's essential to wear sensible shoes when driving the M3W. I do not mean Dr Scholl's clogs, but proper driving shoes or racing boots. This is especially important if you take an outlandish size like me (13EU). I can comfortably drive most normal cars when wearing Doc Marten's footwear, but I found that even my comfortable moccasins did not give me confidence to drive the M3W; and you really do need to feel comfortable and confident when you're behind the wheel of this device.

Between scalp and soles, you do have to wrap up well when the thermometer heads towards the cryogenic zone. In open cars with heaters, all you need in winter is something to keep the top of your head warm, because that is the main exit door for your body heat to escape into the atmosphere. In the M3W, without a heater and with no proper windscreen and no side windows, it's a different matter.

Surprisingly, although I have driven my 3 Wheeler many times in sub-zero temperatures, I have never found that my feet have felt uncomfortably cold. It must be all the tap-dancing on the pedals, I suppose. I do find that my thighs sometimes get somewhat chilled. An old-fashioned motoring rug solves that, but the optional heated seats are worth considering, and the cost is not excessive; I found them useful years ago when the air conditioning/heating system went AWOL in an Audi in the Alps in a chilly winter.

For the top half of the body, it's best to follow motorbiking practice – wear several layers of clothing (you can always remove a layer or two if you start overheating), topped off with a leather jacket, but of course without the back protector, unless you're planning to jump clear.

On cold days, a normal pair of leather driving gloves will be insufficient. You need proper, lined, gauntlets that cover the cuffs of your jacket, otherwise the cold air will shoot up to your exposed armpits.

Chapter eighteen

Are you a Morgan 3 Wheeler type?

I f you've read the book carefully so far and still continue to regard yourself as a potential M3W buyer, then you must have a few components slightly loose, so the answer to the question in the chapter heading is potentially 'Yes.'

The European car market has long been saturated, and volume makers struggle, having to offer more and more while shaving profit margins. The days when German Porsche buyers could specify a car with rubber floor-mats and wind-up windows are, alas, long gone. In France, cars are marketed as 'sur-équipée' (over-equipped), as if this were a virtue. BMW tuner Herbert Hartge, for whom anything on a car that did not improve performance, handling, or driving comfort was superfluous, used to describe this kind of stuff as 'non-stop nonsense.'

Even the most powerful cars these days are very easy to drive at a moderate pace. They don't generally become challenging or even interesting until they are travelling at speeds well above those permitted by the law. They are enormously impressive in many cases, but frustrating and, frankly, rather pointless. This was not the case in the late 1970s, since which time improvements in tyres, brakes, suspension and electronically-controlled safety systems have been radical.

If you like the idea of minimalism in cars as an antidote to all that high-tech overkill, then the M3W might fit the bill. However, it certainly will not appeal to everyone, or indeed – and this is an important point – to everyone's wife. My famously certifiable friend Colin, for example, rather liked the idea of a 3 Wheeler, but admitted that he would never be able to persuade his wife to let him buy one. And he brushed aside my suggestion that he should avoid mentioning the fact that it had a wheel missing; she would undoubtedly notice, he said.

There has been at least one female M3W owner, several wives and girlfriends drive them, and some women are very enthusiastic about them. Others need persuading that purchasing such an impractical device is in some way justifiable, which of course it isn't by any logical argument. If you can cross that barrier by one means or another, you still need to convince yourself that you are compatible with it. There are three basic types of Morgan 3 Wheeler buyer.

In the first group are wealthy people with a garage full of varied stuff, such as a modern Rolls or Bentley, a Ferrari or a Lamborghini, and perhaps also an interesting motorbike or two. A surprising number in this category are present or past owners of TVRs, which perhaps makes them less susceptible to rage or tears when things go wrong, and certainly less surprised.

In the second group are mechanical engineers, who immediately set to work to analyse and modify their M3Ws, and, in many cases, do not hesitate to inform the manufacturer about what's wrong with the product and how it can be improved. The MMC has benefited quite a lot from some of these people, without putting on an excessive display of gratitude.

Finally, there are people like me, neither plutocratic nor engineering geniuses, who muddle along and hope for the best.

There's quite a lot of overlap between the first and second groups. I don't think there is any M3W owner who uses an M3W as a sole, everyday vehicle. It's hard to imagine this being tolerable, or even possible, even with the much-improved 2014 version. In pouring rain it's miserable, with zero visibility to add to the unpleasantness of sitting in a mobile bathtub. On icy roads it must be undriveable, with little grip, and even less traction. It's a car for dry roads and clear days. Some M3W owners are offended by the suggestion that it's a toy. But let's be clear: that is what it is, and there is nothing wrong with that.

So, might you be a potential M3W owner? If you don't immediately say to yourself, 'I want one,' when you see one, the answer is probably negative.

Here's the first question that you should ask yourself: 'Am I a bit mad?' If you answer 'Yes!', then you probably are not mad at all and should instead buy a sensible, practical (and rather nice) two-seater, such as a Mazda MX-5/Miata, which has the same gearbox as the Morgan 3 Wheeler. You'll be pleased to discover that, should you buy the Japanese car, everything works as it should, unless you're exceptionally unlucky; I once had to explain to the Press Director of Mercedes-Benz UK that the vehicle he'd supplied for testing had broken down, without any provocation from the driver. This seemed to be a new concept to him. I became rather angry; eventually, after his mechanics had examined the car, he apologized and agreed that the car had indeed 'broken down.'

If, on the other hand you answer, 'No, I am not mad,' then evidently you are completely barking, and might be a potential Morgan 3 Wheeler owner.

Three events influenced my purchase. One day I was sitting in the shade on a hot day, waiting for my car to be serviced at a BMW dealer near Fréjus in the Var, a French département, when a chap turned up on an unusual-looking motorbike. It sounded like a Harley-Davidson but wasn't. On close inspection, I read the names Buell on the tank and S&S on the engine's timing case. At that stage, I had never heard of either Buell or S&S.

I'm not a biker, and if I were I would not buy a Harley, but I might go for the Buell. You don't have to be a biker to admire the design and exquisite construction of some motorcycles, and that Buell was up there with the best.

Then one day, I was walking the dog and a young chap arrived in a 1920s Amilcar, drifting right and left through an S-bend. Yes, really drifting, not just sliding. I think it was a GCSS, which was probably the model in which the extravagant dancer Isadora Duncan uttered her last word ("SCAAAAAAAARF!") in Nice in 1927. "Affectations can be dangerous", remarked Gertrude Stein aphoristically, when this event was described to her; well, it takes one to know one. Funnily enough, if you like laughing, supposing her latest lover-to-be had been warming her up in a Morgan 3 Wheeler rather than an open-wheeled four-wheeler, Isadora might have been able to carry on her eccentric dancing career for a while longer.

On seeing this Amilcar, I thought, "I'd like one of those," and then I checked the prices and took a deep breath. I also remembered that I might flatteringly describe myself as a below-average mechanic.

The third factor was that my friend Andrew English, *The Daily Telegraph's* Motoring Correspondent, was assembling a Triking, as mentioned in the first chapter. I followed the difficult progress of the modern 3 Wheeler's gestation and finally decided, I've got to have one of those.

The Morgan 3 Wheeler suffered from numerous development problems; despite the factory's best efforts, it's still not a model of dependability. It's also overweight. Official performance figures were absurdly exaggerated, and are still somewhat optimistic. Even in the improved 2014 version, the front suspension geometry is seriously flawed. If you drive hard, the front tyres wear out rapidly.

Self-servicing is not for the faint-hearted. Changing the rear wheel requires special equipment and skills, or a visit to the dealer (your local tyre fitter might not have the necessary skills for the job). The engine is very loud, and numerous other strange noises emanate from other components, some of which may be a cause for concern. The 'roll-over' bars are unlikely to be of much use if you have the misfortune to roll over (the advice is: DON'T EVER DO THAT). The cabin ergonomics leave a lot to be desired. The instruments are junk. Luggage space (unless you purchase the expensive optional luggage rack) is minimal, and the 'boot' is slightly more waterproof than a paper swimsuit. Do you still want one?

Well, I knew a lot of that before I purchased, and I'd guessed much of the rest. Below is a selection of remarks by owners, taken from the TalkMorgan 3 Wheeler forum:

Paul Jacobs, who has owned and competed in Caterham Sevens for more than a quarter of a century, says: "I just love 'off the wall' small performance cars, and I always hankered after a Morgan two- or three-speeder since I was into motorbikes as a kid. Truth be told, I also looked at the Messerschmitt, the Berkeley, even the Bond with the engine over the front wheel when I was 16, and although I did buy a water-cooled two-speeder for £13, I never got it onto the road, and sold it six months later for £15, so I suppose I shouldn't complain."

On the TalkMorgan website, a wide range of reasons is given for purchase, but one theme is common, well expressed by 'R1NGA.' He says he bought his M3W " ... as an antidote to the relentless ethnic cleansing of feel, accessibility and fun from too many modern cars. My last Audi, an RS6, had 540bhp, infinite grip, infinite speed, Veyron brakes, blah, blah, and it became dull and (in the UK at least) totally unusable for the purpose for which it was designed, though I did hit an indicated 200mph on the A1 near Berlin once though, which I admit was quite high up the fun scale ... I was hooked when the M3W was announced, and convinced that it needed a place on the shopping list when *Autocar* tested it. A drive in one following a chat to RTCC in Grazely and my build slot magically appeared ... and then suitable funds sometime later."

'Nippymog' explains that he "... was on the path to buying a touring bike, but the Mrs balked at the idea of riding pillion for long distances. However, I got complete buy-in with the M3W! Rigged out with a biker's electric jacket and gloves, she has completely bought into the idea, even the buying of the recent upgrades which have been a success.

"I would like to think we have a good compromise between bike and car. We get the fresh air, views and fabulous engine noise while in a car. Also, I like the tinker potential with the M3W, which fits right in with my other hobby of model engineering. I don't do heavy car mechanics – that is what the dealer is for – just regular servicing and the pleasure of keeping an attractive piece of engineering in good working order. My 2015 goal is to tour the UK in it."

'TimG' agrees that " ... too much kit and technology on modern cars is removing the fun. It's only a matter of time until it's illegal to open the bonnet unless you are licensed as a dealer." He adds, "It was probably the *Autocar* test that ignited the spark, but I cannot say why it smouldered then for some time, then burst into flame, and I knew I wanted/needed/had to have one. Revolutions were advertising a cancelled order, so I went for a test drive, ordered it, and collected it 19 days later.

"Beside it being the most fantastic fun to drive, you can actually do stuff to it to make it better. I'm sure this is a major factor with many folk. Less equals more fun. I also quite like the look of it. No, actually, I think it looks brilliant."

Chas Saunter's parents " ... were 3-wheeler drivers of the old school, and I often thought of buying an old one. When the five-speed came along it was a no brainer," apart, he admits, from convincing his wife. "For me it is a unique blend of heritage and madness that delivers more fun and smiles per mile than I have experienced with anything else I have owned."

Women played an important role in 'Steve62Hope's' decision: "After 35 years of bikes, then divorce, my new other half did not bond with being on the back of my motorbikes.

"A detour on the way back to work with colleagues after a business meeting to Brands Hatch Morgan got me sorely tempted, but my head ruled until we went on holiday to Cornwall, where a handy signpost to Perranwell Morgan drew me in, and a test drive secured my deposit.

"I used to have a Bond Bug that I rescued from the scrap yard as a student, one hell of a blast till the tipping point when you had to be quick! I always fancied a three-wheeler with the wheels the right way round. I have still got some of the bikes; although with the M3W they are becoming more and more irrelevant and I'll probably concentrate on the 3W."

'Simmo' says: "When I saw it at the Geneva Show I was totally bowled over with the concept, the design, and the overall proposition ... I put down my deposit within a couple of weeks, before any road tests, based on gut instinct that it was going to be a crazy, bonkers fun car. So 90 per cent emotion and 10 per cent rational – the rational bit being I wanted a reliable, everyday usable, less precious alternative to a '30s MG J2." Well, that's what we all hoped for ...

He adds: "It's taken a while to live up to that promise, but the fun bit has always been there, and it's fun that can be accessed without risking your licence ... how many other cars make you grin from ear to ear whenever you take them out for a spin?"

'rolsmith' is a serial three-wheeler man: "Some time back, I came across a website featuring JZRs. I thought they looked amazing, and I finally acquired a Guzzi-powered version. I drove it, wrenched on it, cursed at it, and had a thoroughly enjoyable time.

"When Morgan came out with the new five-speeder, I, along with most of my JZR cohorts, put it down as too expensive, too heavy, and a flash in the pan. I finally realized that no amount of 'fettling' would ever get the JZR on an equal footing with the Morgan. Out came the wallet, in went the deposit, and 18 months later, bingo! Here was a new Morgan in the drive. It also needs a bit of fettling, but I enjoy that sort of thing, and it is a joy to drive!"

Donald Reid ('Donaldosaurus'), who has also owned TVRs among other cars, " ... bought it for the smiles per gallon. Oh, and the wife made me sell the Ducati, so this is as close as I can get, and has more style and practicality than a Scariel Atom. The Caterham did not do much for me before."

After an epic European tour in 2014, Mr and Mrs Reid's M3W broke down in Italy and had to be trailered back to Scotland while they returned separately by train ... and immediately put the beast, a 2012 model with numerous factory upgrades, up for sale. But it was fun while it lasted.

'M3boy' took delivery of his M3W on October 12th 2012. It was " ... a great moment, and a wonderful drive home, only superseded by very many more great runs/drives following that.

"My M3W journey actually started 55 years ago when I was nine! My brothers and I used to cycle to Tilton on the Hill in Leicestershire to watch all the motorcycle scrambles meetings held there. It was fantastic – the sight and sounds live on in my mind today. At every meeting, parked in a farm gateway near the track was a Morgan 3 Wheeler. It was an Aero with an air-cooled JAP engine. We would wait at the end of the scrambles just to see the owner return and roar off – we loved the open valve gear and the sight and sound of this old car!

"I have had lots of cars – Spitfires, Capris, Jaguar, Mercedes, BMWs by the dozen, a Westfield and a JZR, and a lot of bikes too – veteran, vintage and modern. But I always wanted a Mog. I reckoned that I could not afford a '30s car – or have the workshop/skills to keep one fettled and on the road.

"So, to my amazement, when walking up by the start line at Prescott in Spring 2010, there was the new prototype M3W on display – love at first sight! Someone from Morgan fired the job up – and I was hooked!

"However, it was way over my budget – until in the Summer of 2012 I had a couple of unexpected financial windfalls. I worked out if I sold my three bikes, plus the windfalls I could buy an M3W. So I did!

"What fun I have had. I have joined in/entered eight motoring events, including two MTWC events. I have been on numerous local runs all round the Cotswolds – covering over 3000 miles now."

A lot of rectification has been required, including the new uprated wishbones introduced early in development, a new rear drive sprocket, new rectifier and numerous other small mods/upgrades. Nevertheless, "Looking back on all this work, I would say the factory (which is my local dealer) has been brilliant. They have fixed everything promptly and with good spirit – and added lots of work/upgrades which I did not ask for – or even knew needed doing. There have been times when I was in despair at the transmission noises – but I decided to persevere and am glad I did."

For Achim König, a German who divides his time between the Stuttgart area and Brittany, it was love at first sight: "I saw a picture, it said 'Buy me,' so I did. Later on, I found some rational arguments for my decision (never buy new windscreen wipers, never buy anti-freeze for the door locks, next time buy only three instead of four tyres ...) to explain to my friends that I'm not crazy ... but the decision was made earlier."

One buyer, an American, claims to have bought his M3W for practical reasons: "I needed to get back in the HOV lane (killer commute to work)." HOV stands for High Occupancy Vehicle. In California, these highway lanes are designed for use by vehicles containing three or more people, but motorcycles are also allowed to use them.

"Whenever anyone French asks why I bought my M3W, I reply, 'C'est possible que je suis un peu fou,' and I smile at them with the mad staring eyes."

One important piece of advice before taking the plunge: check out how far away your nearest Morgan dealer is, as this could reduce or increase your future misery in direct proportion to the distance. Ideally, you should be within an hour, two at most, from your nearest dealer or service agent. In the south-east and Midlands of England, and on the Welsh borders, this covers most people, but elsewhere you can find yourself a very long way from assistance when things go wrong, as they probably will from time to time.

There is only one Morgan dealer in Scotland (in Perth) and in parts of Europe they are few and far between, especially in the vastness of France. In the USA, there is a scattering of dealers on the eastern side, and one or two in the far west, but if you live in one of the central states, you really need to be your own engineer, or have a skilled mechanic based nearby.

VISIT VELOCE ON THE WEB – WWW.VELOCE.CO.UK
All current books • New book news • Special offers • Gift vouchers • Forum

Chapter nineteen

Morgan: past, present, and, let us hope, future

In 1970, a neatly-inscribed graffito on a low wall in Hornsey, north London, predicted that "CHAIRMAN MAO WILL LIVE FOR 10,000 YEARS." Happily, this proved to be inaccurate, the writer (if not an ironist) failing to appreciate that nothing in the entire universe is forever, except for eternity. Where is Gondwanaland? What happened to the triceratops? How can I book a PanAm flight? And what might the future hold for the Morgan Motor Company of Pickersleigh Road, Malvern Link, Worcestershire, England?

In 1950, there were more than 60 companies in Britain producing motor cars. For some years, the United Kingdom (almost entirely England) was the world's second-largest manufacturer of cars by volume, and for a while it was even the world's leading exporter of cars.

If you'd gone into a betting shop in the early 1950s and asked to place a bet that in 50 years' time only one of those British companies then operating would still exist independently, you could have got a smile and very generous odds. If you had spiced up the wager by adding that that company would be Morgan, you would have received a derisive laugh and probably been given a million to one. Had you slapped down a tenner or two, you would now be a very rich elderly person, if you too had survived to cash in on your extraordinary foresight.

The Morgan Motor Company was already an improbable, eccentric survivor in 1950, and at the beginning of the 21st century it was one of only two car makers in the entire world from the early years of motoring still run by the family that had founded it. The other was Peugeot, maker of the world's best pepper mills. Since then, PSA Peugeot-Citroën has turned pear-shaped, and although it has not turned turtle, it no longer operates as it did only a short time ago, and is now firmly under the thumb of the harsh wind from the East, Dong-Feng. Peugeot family members have become minority shareholders, with some influence but no power. They cannot tell the Chinese what to do next.

If that has happened to Peugeot, among numerous others to suffer similar or worse fates over the years, what hope for the MMC? Can it survive independently, or indeed at all? A few years ago, one might instead have asked "Can it continue to thrive?" but thriving is not something the MMC has done for a while, though the present management expresses confidence in the future.

Making a profit has always been difficult in the motor industry, especially for low-volume car makers lacking the advantage of economies of scale. A larger manufacturer can afford to make a mistake here and there, but not too many or too big. The minnows in the enormous ocean, like Morgan, have to get the product right, or just about right, first time, and that is a hard trick to pull off even if fundamental errors are not made; but to err is human.

It's perhaps worth considering the differences between Peugeot and Morgan. Although the French company has always been far larger, the way the two companies are run has also been very dissimilar. In particular, there was a strict rule at Peugeot, introduced several decades ago, that no family member could be appointed Chief Executive Officer. Over the years, several potentially excellent administrators named Peugeot perhaps felt that they were deprived of the destiny that they deserved, and one or two of them may have been justified in this belief.

The benefit was that the company was protected from destructive intra-family rivalry. This did not mean that there were no disagreements or feuds, of course; the Peugeots are just like any other family, just a lot richer.

The MMC has never had such a prohibition incorporated in its company rules. Harry Morgan was the founder, and he handed the

The main part of the Pickersleigh Road factory, built in 1913, still looks from above much as it did in the early 1920s, but the Morgan Motor company has expanded, and is no longer surrounded by countryside. (Courtesy MMC)

business to his son Peter, who in turn made way for Charles. At the time of writing, Charles still appears (at least to outsiders) to be running the company a century after it had been founded. Charles seems to

believe this. In August 2014, those clicking into his Twitter account and seeing his description of himself as "Charles Morgan of the United Kingdom car manufacturer, Morgan Motor Company Ltd" would

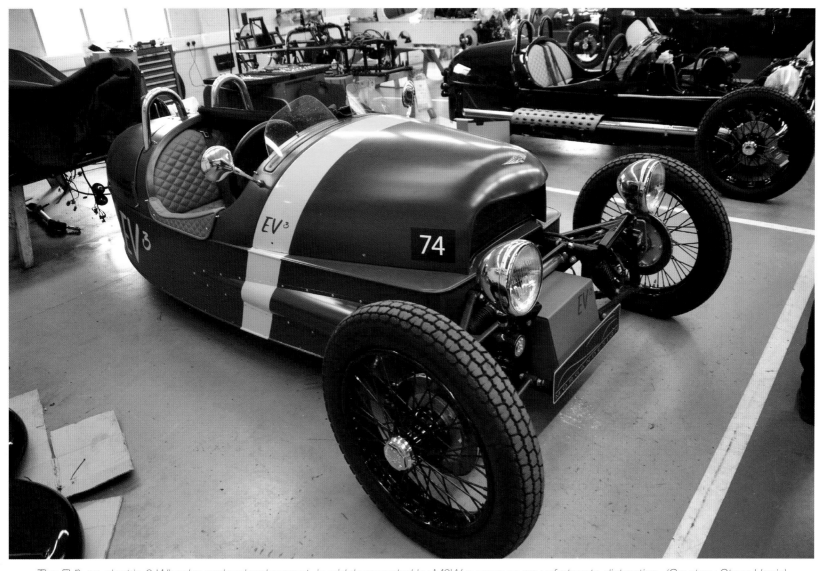

The EV³, an electric 3 Wheeler under development, is widely regarded by M3W owners as an unfortunate distraction. (Courtesy Steve Harris)

naturally imagine that he remained Grand Panjandrum, rather than that he had become merely a non-executive shareholder.

This is not a specific criticism of Charles, but it would probably have been better for both him and the MMC if the Malvern minnow had had a similar rule to that of Peugeot. Naturally, Charles has a sense of entitlement to run the company that shares his name, but that does not necessarily mean that he is the best man for the executive job.

When Sir John Harvey-Jones visited Pickersleigh Road in 1989/1990 to make the *Troubleshooter* programme about the company, Peter Morgan, son of the founder, was already scaling down his involvement (he retired as Managing Director in 1999 but remained Chairman until his death in 2003), and handing control to Charles, who had joined the company in 1985 after a career as a BBC film cameraman.

Although the Morgan family disagreed with many of the conclusions of Harvey-Jones, they and others at the MMC took careful note of some of them. There is no doubt that, while remaining probably the least modern car manufacturer in the world, Morgan addressed many of Sir John's criticisms, and, to give credit where it is due, some of this was down to Charles himself.

The factory became a lighter, brighter place in which to work, and design and production systems became more efficient. More modern tooling was introduced, and the pushing of rolling chassis up and down slopes, which had brought out a fit of Harvey-Jones giggles, was eliminated.

Despite this progress, the situation gives cause for concern. With the benefit of hindsight, it's undeniable that many fundamental and far-reaching errors have been made over the last few years.

At the time of writing it's unclear whether Charles Morgan will succeed in his attempts to wrest back control of the family firm, and it is still a family firm – with or without him at the helm – or what the

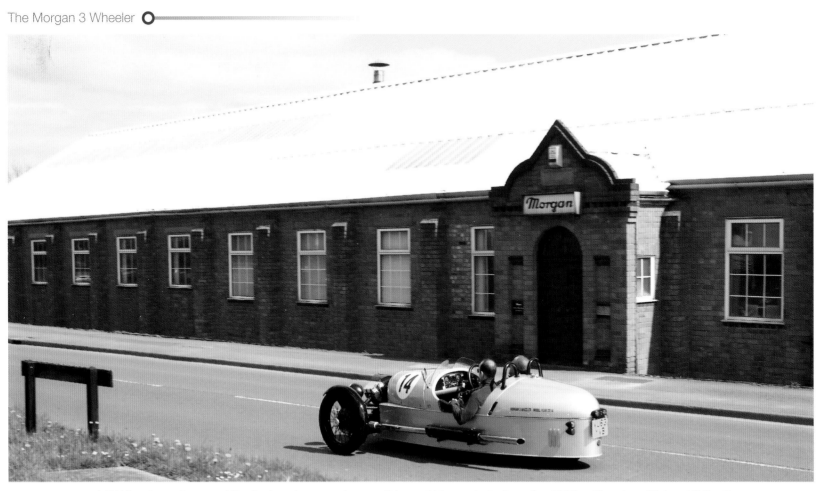

A 3 Wheeler cruises past the factory. In monochrome, this could be a photo from the 1920s. (Courtesy Richard Gilbert)

consequences of that might be, though there would undoubtedly be major changes in senior executive management. However, it seems low in probability. In any case, whoever runs the MMC in future faces the same, numerous, problems, and will have to address them urgently and correctly.

To put it bluntly, the Morgan Motor Company could benefit from a *Troubleshooter*, once again. Sir John Harvey-Jones has gone to another place, and I am not qualified for that role, rather to my relief. Nevertheless, I think I can see fairly clearly what the problems are. It is evident that the MMC is at a stage where it must choose its future direction, and it's a complex dilemma.

A starting point of the analysis of the company as a whole might be a close examination of relations between the factory and its dealer network, which is the lifeblood of any car company. The MMC is not renowned for its communication skills, though Steve Morris told me in August 2014 that every dealer in the world has his mobile telephone number and that his telephone is switched on 24 hours a day. I hope they allow him a few hours' sleep. From what I hear, some dealers are better than others (I have been lucky in this respect).

Beyond that, there is a problem with the sales chain – at times there has been over-production, leading to 'dumping' at substantial

discounts. The spares department needs to be shaken rather than stirred. It is not so much a 'Just In Time' system, rather it is 'Just You Wait.'

And then there's the 3 Wheeler: some of the company's problems directly concern it. However, if the MMC were to fail, which I do not think will happen, it is unlikely to be because of the 3 Wheeler. Rather, it would be the end result of a series of decisions taken a few years ago, each of which must have seemed like a logical step at the time.

The Aero range has been a commercial failure, and was, perhaps, a leap too far, but one can readily see the logic behind its creation: it is a higher-tech car than the traditional Morgans, while retaining hand-crafted elements and a retro look. It was intended as a means of maintaining sales in the USA.

Unfortunately, US regulators moved the goalposts, and now even the Aero cannot meet Federal standards concerning accident safety (even though it's reasonably good in that respect) and emissions. The latter could be resolved, perhaps, with BMW's assistance. The bigger problem is the requirement for smart air-bags, and there's no obvious answer to that.

But even if the Aero could be sold in north America, it's not clear that it could ever return sufficient profit to justify itself. It cost, for a small player in a big business, a fortune to develop, and frankly, in retrospect, it looks like a major strategic error. There are some owners who are pleased with the vehicles, but there are not enough people out there who think an Aero is a more sensible way of spending a stack of money than choosing something like a Porsche, which will never let you down; or so it used to be believed. At least the Aero does not have a tendency to catch fire, which perhaps disqualifies it from classification as a supercar.

Apart from it being the wrong direction for the company, the MMC came out of that process no longer owning the ground on which its cars are made. According to Steve Morris this is not as perilous as it sounds: he says that the MMC's Board retains " ... big control over everything," concerning that. Let's hope so.

There have been several probably unhelpful distractions along the way. The Eva GT project was an extended version of the Aero, while the LIFECar went in the other direction, using a shortened Aero platform. The Eva GT failed to take off at all, after £1.4 million had been spent, again a huge cost for a small company. It was canned because it, too, would have failed to obtain US certification.

The Eva was a serious attempt to maintain Morgan's presence in the lucrative US market. The LIFECar (LI for lightweight, FE for fuel efficient), mentioned in passing in chapter one, was a pipe-dream, though it was originally designed to run on hydrogen rather than hot air.

The project was embarked upon in collaboration with a number of clever and talented people. Cranfield Institute of Technology, Oxford University, Birmingham City University, and Hugo Spowers, the eccentric genius of a company called Riversimple, were all involved. There was government funding for a while. When this ran out in 2011, the powering of the LIFECar had switched from hydrogen fuel cells to the more attainable idea of a petrol/electric hybrid.

The project gradually fizzled out. Riversimple continues to work on a fuel-cell car, but no longer in collaboration with the MMC. In July 2014 you could still find the LIFECar tucked away in the recesses of the MMC's website, where it was suggested that it remained a future production model, while, in the same month, Wikipedia, the worldwide authority on everything, proclaimed that the LIFECar " ... will be available legally in America in 2011." Perhaps it will. Try modifying a DeLorean and see if you can get there by time travel.

Morgan has spent considerable engineering time developing an electric version of the 3 Wheeler, the EV3, which worries many observers.

There is one respect in which the LIFECar may turn out in the long run to have been money and effort well spent, not because of all the complex propulsion technology, but because of its dimensions ...

As is usually the case, it's far easier to analyse what is wrong than to construct solutions that stand a chance of being effective. There are two main schools of thought on what should be done.

The first of these is that the 'trads' (the traditional models – the 4/4, Plus 4, and Roadster) have been neglected in recent years, and that, with a relatively modest investment, they could be adapted to pass the tests for sale in the USA. If the fuel tanks were split into two and moved forward, as in the M3W, if the cars were fitted with current smart-bag technology, and if the chassis were stiffened by turning the outer lip down and increasing the height of the crossmembers, Yankee Doodle Dandy. It sounds simple enough ... I shall come back to that.

In fact, the latest Plus 8, introduced in 2012, represents a halfway house between trads and modern, and is, perhaps, the prototype of four-wheeled Morgans for the next couple of decades. It is an Aero in trad disguise with a bonded aluminium chassis. There may be Roadster, Plus 4 and 4/4 versions in future.

The reason for this is that the real trads, in the face of ever-tightening legislation, probably have a limited shelf life. Therefore, the future lies in using the shortened Aero chassis of the Plus 8, which was first developed in the LIFECar, with the trad styling on top. Whether the resulting vehicles will retain the artisanal appeal of the trads is a key question.

Nevertheless, although the MMC says that there are no plans for the trads to go back on sale in the States, this might rapidly change. In August 2014, new legislation was pending in the USA that would exempt a car such as a Morgan trad (which would be defined as a replica of something from more than 25 years ago) from current safety standards. This would favour a number of specialist brands, such as Caterham, as well as Morgan.

This would be a boon to the MMC. Not being able to sell four-wheelers in North America has lost the company a substantial amount of revenue, and the Board surely does not wish that to continue indefinitely.

Steve Morris says: "There is lobbying going on at the moment, and we have to wait and see what comes of that. There are ways of getting under the radar, but we don't want to do that. We have an important brand name, and we want to keep on the moral high ground. Hopefully the revised legislation will allow us to do it. It can be a bit of an ego trip if you are not careful. The Aero project cost us a fortune."

Regarding the possibility of a short-chassis Aero based on the LIFECar, he says, "The problem is smart air-bags. You go to the specialists in that – Continental, Siemens, Bosch, and you are looking at six figures. But we are looking into it. Never say never."

In the longer term, there's no reason why Morgans must continue with the same engineering concept forever. It is not carved in stone that they must have sliding-pillar front suspension and a live rear axle. The former was quite a clever innovation a century ago, but they are not the Sliding Pillars of Wisdom, and H F S Morgan adapted an existing design rather than invented the concept. At the other end, it's probable that the supply of live axles will dry up some day.

Trad Morgans handle quite well, especially with a few simple modifications, despite these features rather than because of them. I have not driven an Aero or the modern Plus 8. Theoretically, their relatively sophisticated engineering design should give greatly superior handling, but from what I understand, they are essentially almost there, just needing fine-tuning, specifically at the front end.

It is rather a surprise that, although the MMC has highly talented people with various engineering backgrounds working for it, it does not at present have a specialist suspension engineer. There are quick drivers, and then there are quick drivers who can describe accurately what the car is doing, and then, at the rarefied end of the spectrum, there are drivers who can analyse what needs to be done. Morgan needs one of those people, at least to act as a consultant. In the circumstances, it is remarkable that the cars leave the factory handling as well as they do.

Such a specialist would never have allowed the original M3W out of the building, and indeed, as already mentioned, the concept of the revised front suspension on the 2014 model did not originate within the factory, though it was adapted there.

I think it would take a carefully-chosen suspension wizard a relatively short time to transform the independent suspension and steering of the Aero range and its derivatives. There should be a rule that once the specification of a model had been signed off, no changes would be permitted without consulting the consultant. Not having such a rule led TVR onto the wrong path several times, to the great frustration of Rhoddy Harvey-Bailey, one of the great suspension wizards of all time.

More modern underpinnings combined with the traditional look seems to be the way forward. If this works, Charles Morgan will be able to say, "I told you so!" Well, there are two schools of thought about him, too. The first, to which he personally subscribes, is that he is among the great visionaries of the motor industry, and that Morgan is not Morgan without him. Then there is a second view, as suggested in chapter one. Once again, as with the selection of the MMC's future strategy, hindsight will eventually provide an answer.

Getting back on topic, I have some ideas and suggestions about what might be done concerning the thing with a wheel missing (in the literal sense). I shall come back to that in the next chapter. For now, though, it's worth mentioning that if the MMC's 3 Wheeler subsidiary company folded at some point, with or without the failure of the parent company, that would almost certainly not cause the MMC's downfall. It would not prove, to me at least, that boldly returning to where they had gone before had been a bad idea. At the risk of sounding like an apologist for Communism, it was the execution that was wrong, not the idea. Now that the execution is better, the survival chances are consequently much greater.

If the M3W does drop off the perch with a resounding thump, the most likely cause would be, once again, the tightening of US regulations. This is a constant threat for small manufacturers, not only Morgan. There is absolutely no chance, for example, that the 3 Wheeler could be certified for sale anywhere, except perhaps Africa, if it were classified as a car rather than as a motorcycle.

When you're about to take a step in any direction, you have no choice but to start from where you are, even if that happens to be knee-deep in the nitrogenous. I have been skirting around the big question, hinted at in the early part of this chapter: can the MMC successfully implement these changes on its own, while remaining an independent company?

It is always hazardous being a small player in a big game, and it is admirable that the MMC has survived into its second century as the motor industry's coelacanth, but the hazards facing it grow ever greater. In a world of increasingly tight automotive legislation, and with the various internal problems outlined in the previous paragraphs, the only way ahead some observers see for the MMC is a close alliance with or even a takeover by a large international car company.

All at Morgan – especially, but not only the family – will resist this, and probably resent the very suggestion, but being taken over might be the only possible option. Developing new models properly is an expensive process. Provided a new owner respected the essence of Morgan, and understood why it has defied the odds for so long, this would not necessarily be a disaster for those who admire and buy Morgan cars, who are, after all, the most important people for the company.

The ideal partner or parent company would be either BMW, whose engines have been fitted to Morgans for some years, or the VW Group. Both of these corporations include motorcycle divisions, which would probably be useful for the 3 Wheeler, while selective use of the worldwide dealership networks of one of those motor industry giants would supplement Morgan's existing dealer base and provide cover for owners in areas where none presently exists.

However, the chief advantages of such an association, whether it turned out to be a partnership or a full takeover, would, of course, be economies of scale, component-sharing, and access to the most advanced research and development facilities and techniques in the industry.

On the first of these points, if you're ordering components for the production of about 1000 vehicles per year from a supplier, you are obviously not going to get the same unit price as a company manufacturing a few thousand times that number.

To end this analysis on a positive note, I think it is unlikely that Harvey-Jones' dire prediction that Morgan would eventually " ... quietly disappear" (which he later partially retracted) will come to pass: Morgan has a brand image unlike that of any other car company. Morgans are cool and timeless, and they appeal across the generations. All of that is of enormous value. Morgan cars could continue to be both quirky and desirable even if the company fell into the hands of a multinational mega-corporation, but there may be ways of avoiding that. I am sure that the key members of the present management team, Tim Whitworth and Steve Morris, are working hard on this with their engineers.

Chapter twenty

... and the future of the 3 Wheeler

inally, back to Pickersleigh Road and the 3 Wheeler. Whether or not the MMC continues as an independent operator, or becomes a branch of one of the big players, the priority must be to make the little car more reliable. Substantial progress has been made already. The 2014 model was a big improvement over the 2013 model, which was itself vastly better than the first-year cars. Development has not stopped, either.

If a new owner were to take over, I am certain that the 3 Wheeler would form an important part of future plans. In gaining Morgan a lot of valuable publicity, it introduced the marque to a new group of potential customers, not only for the 3 Wheeler itself. It is simultaneously the entry-level model and a 'halo-effect' model. Let us proceed on the premise that our imaginary mega-corporation would maintain the 3 Wheeler in production. And on the subject of premises ...

Having bought back the factory and the land from the banks, a new owner could then turn Pickersleigh Road almost exclusively back to its origins, the manufacture of three-wheeled cars. It would also be a good idea to keep all the wood and leather craftwork for the four-wheelers there. It's vital that these artisanal elements of Morgans should be retained, and especially that the cars should have hand-made ash frames. These processes, rather than the use of sliding pillars, are part of the very essence of Morgan.

For the 3 Wheeler, I would institute an intense analysis of every element of it, the objective being to make the build process more efficient and the end product better, lighter, stronger and, I emphasize again, more reliable. By rushing into production, Morgan failed to get the basics right.

I would keep body production at Premier in Coventry, and chassis fabrication at ABT, because both companies do an excellent job. A further redesign of the chassis, for even greater strength and perhaps some weight loss, might be considered.

I know for certain that, following some avoidable errors, ensuring safe operation of the driveline has been the priority, indeed the obsession, of engineers working on the 3 Wheeler. The entire driveline has been examined in detail, primarily in the quest for improved durability and reliability.

If I were in charge of the 3 Wheeler project, after I had sorted that out, I would next alter the design of the front suspension. The existing, primitive and geometrically unsound system (though in modified form it now works quite well) would be put into early retirement, and its replacement would be fully-adjustable, for toe, camber and castor. The most logical and cost-effective approach would probably be to buy the rights to the Empire Racing Kit (see chapter thirteen). At the very least, this could be offered immediately as a factory-approved dealer option.

At the same time, the steering lock would be improved so that a three-point turn could be made, without spinning up the rear wheel, within an area smaller than a football pitch.

I would look at ways of reducing weight without compromising structural strength. If the Triking is what Colin Chapman might have created had he built a three-wheeler (it's no coincidence that Triking's founder had worked for Lotus), the M3W's spiritual godfather might perhaps be W O Bentley – not only because of the swept volume of the cylinders ...

At an alleged 1156lb (525kg) the M3W is heavier than the MMC had intended. A Swiss owner put his M3W on an official government weighbridge; he received a slip of paper with 535kg printed thereon.

Earlier Morgan three-wheelers were featherweights. The three-speeder (F4) hit the scales at around 350kg. The two-speeders were even lighter. There is no way that the MMC, even presenting the new 3 Wheeler as a motorcycle rather than a car, could get away with such construction.

The essence of the factory; the essence of Morgan.
(Courtesy Blake Marvin/MMC)

No two 3 Wheelers are identical, as this photo shows.
(Courtesy Blake Marvin/MMC)

Could the M3W be lightened significantly? Matthew Welch remarks, "This is a tricky one to answer. It is easy to look at the 3 Wheeler and make many suggestions to save weight, but the materials used and design chosen is there for a reason ... either cost of parts, tooling costs, or, in a lot of cases, for certification requirements. The places that could be looked at may be the rear swing arm, and possibly the rear wheel/ hub assembly ... but these would need lots of testing, tooling and checking ... plus, of course, there would be cost increases, and the price of the 3 Wheelers is quite a sensitive thing ... after all, no one needs a vehicle like this, it's usually a second or third vehicle/toy."

Other improvements would be simpler. A system to move the pedal box for drivers of different heights without having to use a ramp and spanners is one. If Marcos could do it, Morgan surely can.

The luggage compartment should remain dry in a downpour. Rather than using the mudguard system mentioned in chapter fourteen, I would prefer this to consist, as in the basic car, of a single piece of moulded fibreglass – which I would insist at the very least be fixed by a maximum of three screws, rather than nine, and preferably by a single rotating clamp.

The steering wheel would be adjustable for reach and, perhaps, tilt, though the latter might be too expensive. The existing instrument display would be thrown out and the new one would more closely resemble that of the Liberty ACE. There would be no digital readouts. The fuel gauge would give accurate information, and would not suggest that the vehicle is running on air while there are still more than two gallons in the tanks.

The front cowl fixings would be improved. The Dzus fasteners are an elegant solution, but it should be possible to make their operation more satisfactory.

Other optional, factory-fitted extras might include locks for the front cowl and the boot (trunk), and a luggage rack that did not necessitate drilling through the roll-over bars.

One shed of the Malvern Link factory would become a 'skunk works' where a clever team of engineers would think impossible thoughts before breakfast and produce imaginative plans for the future by lunchtime. Nine out of ten might be knocked on the head; I refer to the ideas rather than the engineers.

The first of these projects would be a modification of the existing model, with properly braced, higher roll-over bars. The design brief would be to do this with minimal loss of luggage space.

I would examine the possibility of a body/chassis redesign, to incorporate a proper roll-cage. It could be combined with simple weather protection, possibly including a windscreen with wipers, a hinged rear hatch, and the kind of detachable lightweight lid that TVR used in the 1980s and 1990s.

The aero-screen version would continue as the base model. Fairbourne Carriages' Aero screens could be offered as an optional extra, again through dealers, to keep the factory operation simpler and dealers happy.

The most ambitious project might be an entirely new 3 Wheeler, along the lines of the Volkswagen GX3, but with design elements inspired by the Aero range. I do not envisage this as replacing for the existing 3 Wheeler, but as an addition to the range.

Interestingly, Matthew Welch has similar thoughts. When I asked him the question, without mentioning the GX3, "What would you change if you could start the M3W project all over again?" he first mentioned the compensator problem, and then replied: "I'd like to have a single-sided rear swing-arm design looked at. This could make removal and fitting the rear wheel much easier, and also make adjusting the rear belt a less delicate procedure to get right.

"A bit of a pipe dream I suppose, but I would also like to see what an all-new 21st century 3 Wheeler could look like: aluminium bonded chassis, water cooled engine, and some modern styling. I think it would be an interesting concept to look at if nothing else ... but it would still need to be unquestionably a Morgan 3 Wheeler. Many others have tried, but no one else has managed to make anything

Italian designer/illustrator Claudio Bardeggia imagined this Morgan-inspired Caterham three-wheeler. The rollover bar design could be adapted by Morgan without losing much luggage space (Courtesy Claudio Bardeggia)

A single swinging rear arm, as on the stillborn VW GX3, would remove a lot of hassle for M3W owners.

close to a real Morgan 3 Wheeler, be it a car from the 1930s or a 2014 Morgan 3 Wheeler."

In many respects, this describes the GX3, including the single-sided rear swing arm.

Supposing, on the other hand, the MMC is not taken over, and manages to survive on its own. There's still a strong chance that this can happen. In that case, the management must concentrate on the basics. As far as the MMC in general is concerned, there are discontented dealers. With the 3 Wheeler, there are also many discontented customers. The reasons for this discontent have been explained in some detail in this book, and they need to be addressed urgently. I am sure that Steve Morris and his team are fully aware of that.

I very much hope that the M3W will continue to bring excitement to new owners – and let them down far less than happened with the early versions. I am confident that that is possible. Believe me, the 3 Wheeler is just about the most exciting vehicle I have ever driven. It also attracts attention more than anything else. As one Morgan four-wheeler owner

put it, when he was driving in convoy with a 3 Wheeler it was as if he were " ... wearing a cloak of invisibility."

An interesting point to note is that in mid-2014, a number of 3 Wheeler owners were trading in their vehicles for four-wheeled trad Morgans, mostly the 4/4 but also some Plus 4s. I began setting this process in motion for myself in July 2014, and I hope that by the time you read this I will have my nearly-new 4/4, kitted out to my specification.

The theory behind this is that the trads provide what we hoped for from our crazy purchase: a classic-car type of driving experience combined with mechanical components that make the vehicle almost as reliable as a Volkswagen Golf. As one contributor to the TalkMorgan forum sarcastically pointed out, the 4/4, which holds the world record for continuous production, is reliable because they have had nearly 80 years to sort it out.

In view of my previous record in these things, there will almost certainly be a massive worldwide recall of Golfs shortly after this book goes to press, but the point stands. I confess that my decision

It is not hard to imagine the GX3 redesigned to be a Morgan: the 21st century successor to the F2.

motoring to many people who had never previously considered such eccentric behaviour (most 3 Wheeler owners had not previously been Morganists), but who looked at the trads when at their dealerships and noticed light weight, sufficient but not enormous power, relatively narrow tyres, old-fashioned but sturdy (and tuneable) suspension, and thought ... that could be fun ...

There are also some doughty owners of early 3 Wheelers who, having got through a difficult and frustrating ownership experience, are trading in their 2012 or 2013 models for the latest version, and there are others who are considering doing so. Once bitten, twice barmy, you may say, but the word has spread about improved reliability.

In these final two chapters, playing Devil's Advocate, I have speculated on what might happen to the Morgan Motor Company. Provided it gets its act together, the Malvern manufacturer can remain independent, and the 3 Wheeler, an admirably brave undertaking, can have a long and successful future.

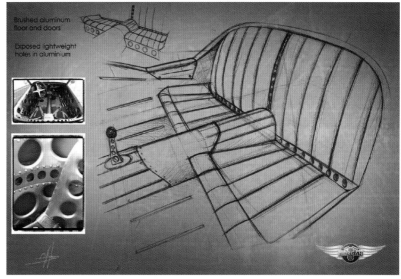

An interesting early study by Matt Humphries for the M3W's interior. Special versions such as this could be profitable for the MMC. (Courtesy MMC)

was also strongly based on a lack of confidence in myself as a mechanic.

If it has done nothing else, Morgan's 21st century reversion to the concept of its founder will have introduced four-wheeled Morgan

VISIT VELOCE ON THE WEB – WWW.VELOCE.CO.UK
All current books • New book news • Special offers • Gift vouchers • Forum

137

If you do not look at this photo and say to yourself, 'I want one of those!' then you will probably never be a Morgan 3 Wheeler person.

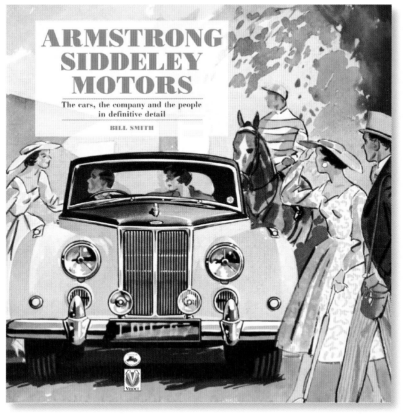

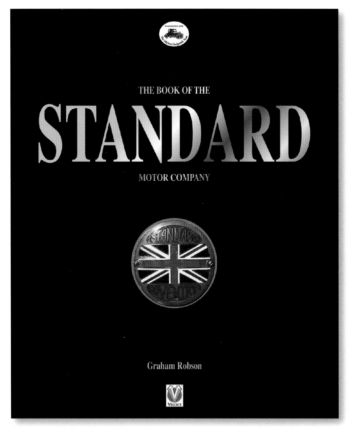

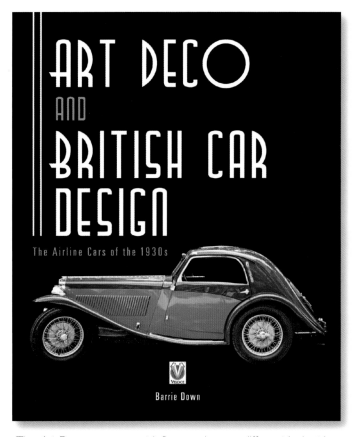

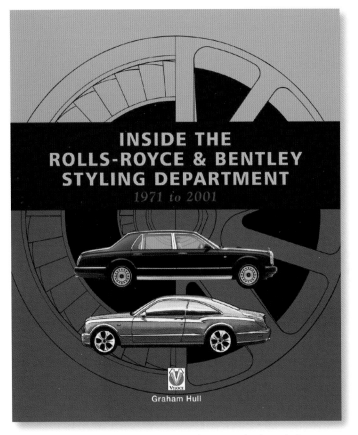

Index